PAPA

AN INTIMATE BIOGRAPHY OF MARK TWAIN

D0125309

Books by CHARLES NEIDER

Fiction

NAKED EYE
THE AUTHENTIC DEATH OF HENDRY JONES
THE WHITE CITADEL

Nonfiction

BEYOND CAPE HORN: TRAVELS IN THE ANTARCTIC
EDGE OF THE WORLD: ROSS ISLAND, ANTARCTICA
SUSY: A CHILDHOOD
MARK TWAIN
THE FROZEN SEA: A STUDY OF FRANZ KAFKA

Edited by Charles Neider

THE SELECTED LETTERS OF MARK TWAIN
THE COMIC MARK TWAIN READER
A TRAMP ABROAD, BY MARK TWAIN
THE AUTOBIOGRAPHY OF MARK TWAIN
THE COMPLETE SHORT STORIES OF MARK TWAIN

Susy and Papa in an impromptu charade

PAPA

AN INTIMATE BIOGRAPHY OF

MARK TWAIN

by Susy Clemens

HIS DAUGHTER, THIRTEEN

With a Foreword and

Copious Comments by Her Father

NOW PUBLISHED IN ITS ENTIRETY
FOR THE FIRST TIME A CENTURY LATER

EDITED WITH AN INTRODUCTION BY

Charles Neider

DOUBLEDAY & COMPANY, INC.
GARDEN CITY, NEW YORK
1985

Library of Congress Cataloging in Publication Data
Clemens, Susy, 1872–1894.
    Papa, an intimate biography of Mark Twain.
    "Now published in its entirety for the first time a
century later."
    Summary: A biography of Twain written by his daughter
Susy when she was thirteen and he was fifty. Includes
correspondence between the two.
    1. Twain, Mark, 1835–1910—Biography. 2. Authors,
American—19th century—Biography. 3. Children's
writings, American. [1. Twain, Mark, 1835–1910.
2. Authors, American. 3. Children's writings]
I. Twain, Mark, 1835–1910. II. Neider, Charles,
1915–   . III. Title.
PS1331.C49   1985   818'.409 [B] [92]   85-6782
ISBN 0-385-23245-4

To my own Susy

Acknowledgments

In addition to the acknowledgments made on the copyright page, I am grateful to the following for their kindness and help in the making of this volume:

Edmund Berkeley, Jr. (Curator of Manuscripts and University Archivist, University of Virginia Library); C. Sally Daly and Marianne J. Curling (Mark Twain Memorial, Hartford); Leo Dolensky (Manuscripts Librarian, Bryn Mawr College); Catherine Doyle; Judy Enteles (Archivist's office, Barnard College); Robert H. Hirst (editor of the Mark Twain Papers, Bancroft Library of the University of California, Berkeley) and Dahlia Armon (editorial assistant, Mark Twain Papers); Robert A. Hull (Manuscripts Department, University of Virginia Library); Harold Kuebler (Doubleday & Company, Inc.); Frank K. Lorenz (Special Collections Librarian, Hamilton College); John Lowrance; Joan M. Neider; Mark Neider; David Roush; Diana Royce (Stowe-Day Foundation, Hartford); Linda Rogers Safran and Olga Weiss (Harper & Row); Silvia Saunders; Walter Teller; David Tewksbury (Hamilton College); Richard A. Watson and Edward J. Willi (Mark Twain Foundation); and Olivia Wood.

I am particularly thankful to Thomas Tenney, editor of the *Mark Twain Journal*, who brought to my attention the series of letters from Olivia (Susy) Clemens to Louise Brownell, who read the present Introduction, and who graciously performed other favors as well.

Contents

List of Illustrations

PAPA

AN INTIMATE BIOGRAPHY OF MARK TWAIN

Introduction

by Charles Neider

This is being written in 1985, the great Mark Twain celebratory year—the 150th anniversary of his birth (November 30, 1835), the 75th of his death (April 21, 1910), and the centenary of the American publication of *Adventures of Huckleberry Finn* (February 1885). It is also the centenary of Susy Clemens's biography of her father, begun when she was thirteen and he was fifty, at the height of his powers, living with his family in the famous and luxurious and unusual (one might even say quaint) house on Farmington Avenue in Hartford.

Before we see Clemens at fifty from the point of view of his adolescent daughter, let's briefly regard him as he appeared to an astute, observant, gifted contemporary, his friend William Dean Howells, who, in his book *My Mark Twain* (1910), wrote, "Clemens was then hard upon fifty, and he had kept, as he did to the end, the slender figure of his youth, but the ashes of the burnt-out years were beginning to gray the fires of that splendid shock of red hair which he held to the height of a stature apparently greater than it was, and tilted from side to side in his undulating walk. He glimmered at you from the narrow slits of fine blue-greenish eyes, under branching brows, which with age grew more and more like a sort of plumage, and he was apt to smile into your face with a subtle but amiable perception, and yet with a sort of remote absence; you were all there for him, but he was not all there for you."

Susy's biography gives a uniquely intimate portrait of Clemens, views of him not seen elsewhere, and proves what had been said about her by her father and some of his contemporaries: what an unusual, wise, observant person she was, and what a loss it was she died so early, at twenty-four (of spinal meningitis). Among other things, it contains letters from her father to her; a description of a visit she and her father made to General Grant (Clemens was Grant's publisher, and Grant was dying of throat cancer); reports of family performances of *The Prince and the Pauper;* her opinions of *Tom Sawyer* and *Huckleberry Finn;* and a charming, surprising description of Clemens reading a book. I quote from her biography, retaining her punctuation.

"The other day, mamma went into the library and found papa sitting there reading a book, and roaring with laughter over it; she asked him what he was reading, he answered that he hadn't stopped to look at the title of the book.' and went on reading, she glanced over his shoulder at the cover, and found it was one of his own books."

About five years after Susy's death in 1896 Clemens noted in his own hand in her manuscript, "That is another of Susy's unveilings of me. Still, she did not garble history but stated a fact."

Jean Clemens was the baby of the family (she was five in July 1885), and she often begged her father to tell her a story, the subject of which she herself insisted on providing. It sometimes strained him to oblige but he did. Later Susy would pump Jean to get the stories for her biography. The results are precious and hilarious. I leave it to the reader to judge if I am exaggerating.

There are many other memorable things in the biography. In January 1885, when Susy was still twelve (she wasn't thirteen until mid-March), Clemens wrote a letter to her from Chicago that shows how much he regarded her as a person able and willing to assume certain adult responsibilities. Susy copied the letter into her biography, spelling incorrectly in two instances. Clemens addresses her as "Susie." This was his early spelling of her name. Soon he would regularly end her name with a *y*.

"Susie dear, Your letter was a great pleasure to me. I am glad you like the new book *[Huckleberry Finn]*; and your discription of its effect on Daisy is all that the most exacting and praise-hungry author could desire. And by the way this reminds me to appoint you to write me two or three times a week in mamma's place; and when you write she must *not* write. What I am after is to save *her*. [His wife, Livy, was frequently an invalid.] She writes me when she aught to be resting herself after the heavy fatigues of the day. It is wrong. It must be stopped. You must stop it.

"When it is your day to write and you have been prevented, see to it that the day passes without a letter, *she* must not write a line. Goodbye sweetheart

"Papa"

Another letter from Clemens in Chicago, written early the following month, reveals his endless and endearing curiosity about people, and his willingness, perhaps eagerness, to share examples of it with Susy. Again she copied it into her biography.

". . . In this hotel (the Grand Pacific) there is a colored youth who stands near the great dining room, and takes the hats off the gentlemen as they pass into dinner and sets them away. The people come in Shoals and sometimes he has his arms full of hats and is kept moving in a most lively way. Yet he remembers every hat, and when these people come crowding out, an hour, or an hour and a half later he hands to each gentleman his hat and never makes any mistake. I have watched him to see how he did it but I couldn't see that he more than glanced at his man if he even did that much. I have tried a couple of times to make him believe he was giving me the wrong hat, but it didn't persuade him in the least. He intimated that *I* might be in doubt, but that *he knew*.

"Goodbye honey

"Papa"

And there is some brilliant, awesome nature writing by Clemens in one of his letters to Susy, this one from Toronto in the middle of February. I'm still quoting from her biography.

"I went toboganing yesterday and it was indiscribeable fun. It was at a girls' college in the country. The whole college—51 girls, were at the lecture the night before, and I came down off the platform at the close, and went down the aisle and overtook them and said I had come down to introduce myself, because I was a stranger, and didn't know any body and was pretty lonesome. And so we had a hand shake all around, and the lady principal said she would send a sleigh for us in the morning if we would come out to the college. I said we would do that with pleasure. So I went home and shaved. For I didn't want to have to get up still earlier in order to do *that;* and next morning we drove out through the loveliest winter landscape that ever was.

"Brilliant sunshine, deep snow everywhere, with a shining crust on it—not flat but just a far reaching white ocean, laid in long smoothe swells like the sea when a calm is coming on after a storm, and every where near and far were island groves of forest trees. And farther and farther away was a receding panorama of hills and forests dimmed by a haze so soft and rich and dainty and spiritual, that it made all objects seem the unreal creatures of a dream, and the whole a vision of a poets paradise, a veiled hushed holy land of the imagination.

"You shall see it some day. . . ."

There is also something dreadfully sad and wonderfully eloquent in the present volume. I have no fear that my mentioning it now will prove to be an anticlimax for the reader, for it can stand being read many times over. On June 26, 1886, Susy writes, "We are all of us on our way to Keokuk to see Grandma Clemens, who is very feeble and wants to see us pertickularly Jean who is her name sake. We are going by way of the lakes, as papa thought that would be the most comfortable way." On July 4th she makes her final entry in the biography. "We have arrived in Keokuk after a very pleasant." That is all. And Clemens writes:

"So ends the loving task of that innocent sweet spirit—like her own life, unfinished, broken off in the midst. Interruptions came, her days became increasingly busy with studies and work, and she never resumed the biography, though from time to time she gathered materials for it. When I look at the arrested sentence that ends the little book, it seems as if the hand that traced it cannot be far—is gone for a moment only, and will come again and finish it. But that is a dream; a creature of the heart, not of the mind—a feeling, a longing, not a mental product: the same that lured Aaron Burr, old, gray, forlorn, forsaken, to the pier, day after day, week after week, there to stand in the gloom and the chill of the dawn gazing seaward through veiling mists and sleet and snow for the ship which he knew was gone down—the ship that bore all his treasure, his daughter."

As I'm sure the reader will agree, the combination of Susy's biography and her father's comments on it, the latter written and dictated in 1901 and 1906, respectively (clearly Clemens was planning to include parts of her biography in his autobiography, together with his comments about her and her biography), is a moving narrative of a wonderful relationship, a sort of love affair, between a father and his daughter. In this case both of the persons were remarkable. Yet granted they were, something universal emerges from the narrative, some exaltation on reading it, a sense that the book may be larger than an intimate portrait of the two chief actors, that just possibly it's an unusual, loving, powerful, moving, revealing portrait of other father-daughter relationships—simply (and most complexly) that.

Although Clemens at first planned to publish his autobiography posthumously (at least so he said), he was persuaded (or persuaded himself) to publish a number of chapters of it in twenty-five installments of the *North American Review* of 1906 and 1907, some of which included excerpts of Susy's biography. This was the first introduction of the biography to the public. Albert Bigelow Paine, Clemens's friend, official biographer and literary executor, had access to the biography when he wrote his three-volume biography of Mark Twain, published in 1912. In the second volume he quoted some 1,700 words of the biography, or 8.8 percent of the original. (I estimate the biography to be 19,200 words long.) In 1924 he published *Mark Twain's Autobiography* in two volumes, in the second quoting approximately 5,750 words (30 percent). In my own edition, *The Autobiography of Mark Twain* (1959), I used 1,100 words (5.7 percent). And *Susy and Mark Twain* (1965), edited by Edith Colgate Salsbury, used some 7,800 words (40 percent). *The North American Review* used about 8,300 words (43.2 percent). These have been the major uses of the biography. Snippets have appeared here and there, for example in *The Annotated Huckleberry Finn*, edited by Michael Patrick Hearn.

Now, although parts of Susy's biography have already been printed, I can assure the reader that there are beautiful, intimate, wondrous events, insights, emotions, and thoughts which have never seen the light of publication and which are included here for the first time. The manuscript of the biography resides in the Manuscripts Department of the University of Virginia Library, specifically in the Clemens Collection in the Clifton Waller Barrett Library of American Literature there. I asked the Manuscripts Department to send me a photocopy of the manuscript, and was told that the manuscript was accompanied by fifty-two footnotes by Clemens—an intriguing piece of information. When I opened the UPS package about a fortnight later and saw how much Mark Twain material there actually was, stacked on top of the biography (in his own hand; I can truly call some of it copious), I was startled and delighted, for I immediately saw that much of it too had never been published. The biography and Clemens's interspersed comments on it have never previously been published in their entirety despite the fact the published parts are wonderful. The present volume would make an unusual publication in any year. In this celebratory year the timing is especially apt.

As to the care and accuracy with which the biography has previously been used. Susy's mistakes in spelling, punctuation, grammar, and consistency are absolutely delicious, and I thoroughly agree with Clemens that to correct them would be to profane them. The *North American Review* sometimes reproduced her quaint spelling or capitalization or punctuation, and sometimes didn't. I wasn't able to discover a pattern. The cause of the discrepancies was probably sloppiness in the preparation of the typescript handed over to the *Review*. Paine, in both his biography of Mark Twain and in his *Mark Twain's Autobiography*, took many liberties with Susy's manuscript, omitting things, correcting spelling, grammar, and so on. He was inconsistent and whimsical, for at times he left her spelling intact, and at others, even when insisting in print that he was retaining her spelling and punctuation, he took silent liberties with them. As for myself in *The Autobiography of Mark Twain*, I too was guilty of infringements, although unlike Paine's mine were involuntary, for I wasn't working with Susy's original manuscript but rather with Clemens's autobiographical dictations in Berkeley, which were in typescript form, or was relying on Paine or the *North American Review*.

Salsbury used patches of the biography out of their

original sequence in a freewheeling way convenient to her book's design (a series of "family dialogues" made up of quotations), and although she seems to have had access to the original manuscript located in Charlottesville (at any rate she ascribed quotations from it on at least eight occasions), she stitched quotations like a crazy-quilt pattern chiefly from several other sources, the great majority of them printed ones—Paine's biography, his *Mark Twain's Autobiography*, my *The Autobiography of Mark Twain*, the *North American Review*, and, in at least one instance, a manuscript in the Mark Twain Memorial in Hartford. As for accuracy, the extent to which she deviated from Susy's manuscript depended almost entirely on the accuracy of her sources, which we have already examined.

In the present volume I had a typescript made from the manuscript, emphasizing to the typist that I didn't want Susy's mistakes corrected, because I treasure them. An unusually good typescript resulted. I then myself compared it with the manuscript and restored certain of Susy's errors which almost inevitably had been corrected. The text now presented is as authentic as I personally have been able to make it. I have gathered Clemens's Foreword from sketches of Susy quoted from *The Autobiography of Mark Twain*, and have not rearranged their order.

Perhaps it is not irrelevant to note that part of my intense interest in the current project may be connected with the fact that I had a delightfully close relationship with my daughter during her earliest years and that I published a biography of her first four years, titled *Susy: A Childhood* (1966), which I hope to conclude with a volume covering her fifth and sixth years.

*　*　*

If we include Clemens's Foreword, we have in the present volume a vivid picture of Susy's life up to the age of fourteen, when she left off writing the biography. All the world knows of her untimely death in the summer of 1896 and its immense impact on Clemens, and his remarkably eloquent, heart-breaking response to it. There were four great, tragic blows in his life: the death of his younger brother Henry in the explosion of the *Pennsylvania,* a Mississippi steamboat; the death of Susy; the death of Livy, his wife; and the death of Jean, his daughter. But Susy's death may have been the cruelest blow of all, for she was still young, hadn't lived her life. Livy had *had* a life, even though mostly as an invalid, she had had children, a loving husband, she was fifty-eight and a half at her death, and had been married thirty-four years.

What of Susy's life between the time she wrote the biography and her death? We know that she lived the normal life (if it may be called normal) of the favorite child of a successful, famous genius. Are there any surprising, startling revelations to be made? I believe there are, amounting to a whole dimension of her life which has received almost no public attention until now. We know that in the years 1890–94, when Clemens was increasingly in financial trouble, crises that led finally to the bankruptcy of his publishing firm, and when he made many anxious business trips between Europe (where his family lived) and the United States, there were the following significant events in her life.

She went briefly to Bryn Mawr College, left for reasons still unclear, accompanied her family to Europe after her parents closed down the Hartford house be-

Susy at Bryn Mawr

cause they could no longer afford to live in it (or the style they were accustomed to while living in it), was vaguely unwell in Europe, discontent, ate foolishly at times, so that she grew thin, occasionally felt faint, gave the appearance of being frail and perhaps *was* frail, suffered from nervousness, malaise, boredom, occasional depression, much insomnia, and at times, while taking singing lessons, was embarrassingly breathless for unspecified reasons. On the other hand there were the "high" times: exultation, real happiness—for no apparent cause.

We know too of Clemens's uneasiness when she went off to Bryn Mawr in the fall of 1890 (she was eighteen), and his excuses to visit her from time to time, and for a while her homesickness at college, and how she came to like Bryn Mawr, and how her classmates discovered she had a fine soprano voice, and how she sang the part of Phyllis in a student performance of *Iolanthe* there, and how—frail, blond, attractive—she gave the impression of being "ethereal" to some of them.

Clemens in a letter to his sister Pamela, October 12, 1890: "The last time I saw her [Susy] was a week ago on the platform at Bryn Mawr. Our train was moving away, and she was drifting collegeward afoot, her figure blurred and dim in the rain and fog, and she was crying." Clemens in a letter to William Dean Howells, February 10, 1891: "Mrs. Clemens has been in Philadelphia a week at the Continental Hotel with Susy (who to my regret is beginning to love Bryn Mawr) and I've had to stay here [Hartford] alone."

A sophomore schoolmate of Susy's, later Mrs. Charles M. Andrews, recalled her as being "very emotional, high-strung, temperamental," and in a letter of February 1949 to Dixon Wecter wrote, "At the time it seemed to us very natural that Olivia [as Susy was known to her classmates; Susan was her middle name] like ourselves should be coming to college, but later I realized how strong was the tie between her and her father, how much they minded being separated, and also how eager Mrs. Clemens was that Olivia should be happy in a new environment, leading an independent life of her own as a college student among girls of her own age, free from the limiting influences of home. . . . Mrs. Clemens would come down occasionally for a short stay, I think in order to keep Mr. Clemens from coming, because she told me that he would make anything an excuse, even to bringing down Olivia's laundry!"

And then there was the time when Clemens was invited to come to Bryn Mawr to give a lecture in the late afternoon of March 23, 1891, and Susy begged her father not to include his famous ghost story, "The Golden Arm," because, as she remarked to a schoolmate, she didn't think it was appropriate for "the sophisticated group at Bryn Mawr," and he promised he wouldn't, but told the story anyway, making the audience jump with fright at the end, as he always successfully made audiences jump. Susy trembled through his telling it and left the chapel before its conclusion and went to a large classroom across the hall, the door of which was open, where she wept because of the broken promise. He found her there and made an excuse and apologized. His excuse was that he could think of nothing, when the moment came, except her voice asking him to promise *not* to tell the story, and rather than allow himself to be tongue-tied on stage he told it.

And we know that she left Bryn Mawr soon after. Exactly when I don't know. Edith Salsbury in *Susy and Mark Twain* says that Livy took her home in the first week of April, but I have a photocopy of an envelope addressed by Susy to Louise Brownell in New York and postmarked Bryn Mawr, Pa., April 20, 1891. Why did Susy leave? Was she ill? Homesick? Upset by her father's lecture? Was Clemens in too tight financial straits now to afford her tuition and board? Hardly likely, given the style in which the family were soon to be living in Europe. Were her parents afraid to leave her alone at college? If so, why? Did she fear being left behind in the States while the rest of the family moved to Europe? We know of Clemens's jealousy of Bryn Mawr because the college separated him from her, and of his remark in his notebook* "Bryn Mawr began it. It was there that her health was undermined." Cryptic enough. No attempt at an explanation as to how her health was undermined. What "health" did he mean? Physical? Mental? Emotional?

And so what is the added dimension I have alluded to? It is revealed in a series of some forty letters from her (as Olivia, not Susy) to a Bryn Mawr classmate, Louise Brownell, which are part of the Saunders Papers in the Hamilton College Library in Clinton, New York. The letters indicate without question a profound relationship between Olivia and Louise Brownell, and one that was passionate, regardless of the extent to which it was or wasn't platonic. It is difficult, it is treacherous, to extrapolate a deep friendship between two young women of the Nineties to today. Whether the relationship was sublimated, or to what extent, I leave to the reader to judge. But of the profundity (at least on Olivia's part), the vast meaning of the relationship to her, a significance which gave her a reason for *being* in those difficult European years, I have no doubt. The correspondence dates from April 1891 (the month Susy left Bryn Mawr) to November 1893, and contains one letter—a dreadful, awful, pathetic, painful one—from the summer of 1894. Let me present some evidence.

Olivia to Louise, October 2, 1891 (one of the very

* *Mark Twain's Notebook*, edited by A. B. Paine (New York: Harper & Bros., 1935).

few letters she dated), from Ouchy, Switzerland: "I think of you these days, the first of college. If I could only look in on you! We would sleep together tonight— and I would allow you opportunities for those refreshing little naps you always indulged in when we passed a night together."

In an undated letter postmarked Lucerne, October 6, 1891, and received at Bryn Mawr on October 15, written on stationery of the Hotels Schweizerhof & Luzernerhof, she begins, "My darling I do love you so and I feel so separated from you. If you were here I would kiss you <u>hard</u> on that little place that tastes so good just on the right side of your nose."

In a letter dated October 31, 1891, beginning "Louise beloved," the ending is, "I love you night and day with all my might. You are so sweet, dear, so lovely lovely! Goodby my darling, Your Olivia.

"I have to go out soon and this is hurried. Oh, Louise if I could only see you! I am so afraid—

"<u>Don't forget me</u>!"

In a letter from the Hotel Royal, Berlin, postmarked March 17, 1892, and received at Bryn Mawr on March 29: "Oh dear but it <u>is</u> good to hear from you again! I had begun to be afraid you had forgotten your own 'hot peanut.' "

A letter postmarked Venice, May 17, 1892, and received at Bryn Mawr on May 29 contains "I throw my arms around you and kiss you over and over again. I hope you are happy and not depressed. I love you with all my heart and more every day. How sweet you are, how lovely you are my dearest!—please write soon to <u>Your Olivia</u>"

Susy in Florence, Italy, in 1892

A letter beginning <u>Villa Viviani</u> and postmarked Florence, June 12, 1893, and stamped in New York on June 21:

"My dearest Louise;

"We are in the chaos of packing as Mlle. L.* and I leave for Paris tomorrow. The rest go on to Munich the next day. I had hoped to get off without a regret but I'm

* A young Frenchwoman who served as a companion and French teacher for Susy in Florence.

not succeeding at all. The look of <u>home</u> has vanished away from the place and it has turned strange and barren. Tomorrow night I shall be in <u>new</u> quarters and the thought makes me <u>ill</u>! Yesterday we dined on the terrace and saw the sun sink behind Florence. I thought of you and how beautiful you would find it. The light on the hills was exquisite and the city was that pale wan violet which it so often takes at sunset. I was sorry to think of going then.

"I had a lovely letter from you the other day. Of course you have been busy. I understand. As for your spirituality weakening from 'disuse' I don't believe that, my beloved! Your spirituality is the largest part of you, and that will not subordinate itself.—Yes I want I <u>want</u> to hear of <u>you</u> tell me everything and I will do all I can in return. You say my letters have been 'vague' lately and I rather suspected this might be the case. But the truth is that what I would <u>tell</u> you of myself will not go on paper. It is quite out of the question but it will keep. In general since you want to know, I am rather discontented and unhappy for varius reason [sic] and I don't seem to have enough 'raison d'etre.' Now I have told my share, for you know dear love that altho' there is a great <u>possibility</u> of intimacy between us, we have never really been <u>intimate</u> yet. We will be some day when it comes natural but at present I do not feel that I know anything about you except that you are altogether beautiful and loveable and <u>perfect</u>. As to what your struggles, and trials and pleasures may be, these are still unknown to me. I <u>love</u> you more than anyone else and yet of your <u>life</u> I seem to know so little! Of course all this is greatly due to our having been so much apart. I <u>do</u> regret it for I think it makes our relations a trifle unnatural. I would rather you knew my sins all of them and my trials too but since they are both rather strange and vulgar, I am not sure that you wouldn't be shocked by them. When we come together dear Louise we will find that we stand just as much at the <u>beginning</u> with each other as the first day we met in B.M.

"I say all this because I am afraid we may run the risk of taking for granted that there is no ground to be gone over between us, whereas there is so much, and this would surely cause a great incompleteness somewhere.

"I love you so very much and I <u>do</u> hope we shall meet soon, but the prospect doesn't look near to me, somehow.

"Please send me a letter as early as you can and tell me that this one of mine hasn't displeased you. I never want to displease you, you must have felt all I have said, <u>yourself</u>.

"With my best love
"Your own

                                        "Olivia

"address
"Drexel & Harjes"

Another letter, no date, the envelope postmarked Franzensbad but the date missing (the stamp was removed), the reverse side postmarked New York, August 11, 1893, so the letter was probably mailed in Franzensbad late July or early August.

"My beloved;
"Your beautiful letter from Chicago has come at last after this long long dreary waiting. It brings you

quite near again and makes me happy. This time of silence has been hard to bear. I have thought of you and longed for you so much lately. Oh my beloved I cannot tell you how precious you are to me! Your letter is beautifully reassuring and makes me resolve never again to be afraid about our friendship. In fact I don't think I ever am <u>deeply</u> afraid and yet I wish that when I see you I could just slip into your room and take you in my arms without any questioning between us, as if we had never been apart. I believe that then I should be perfectly happy, my own darling. But I am sure that there are many things in me which you will object to. Nevertheless as you suggest I will 'trust' and not 'analyse'. I have with me a constant sense of your loveliness, and sweetness, and I can never be grateful enough that I possess your love.

"Many things have happened since I wrote last which I am afraid was way back in Florence. I went to Paris to see Marchesi* and spent a month there with Mlle L. We were in a nice French family out near the Bois and had a very pleasant time for Paris is enchanting in June. Marchesi said some pleasant and unexpected things about my voice but insisted she could do nothing with me in my present state of health. From there I went to the family in Munich and Clara and I came together after our long separation. Then we all hurried down to Hölz where I staid two weeks and then left for this Godforsaken spot where I must remain six weeks with a dreadful German old maid as companion. After that it will be St. Moritz or the sea or both. In

* A voice teacher who came from an Italian family of singers and voice teachers. Susy hoped to have a career as an opera singer. Clemens sometimes wondered if she wouldn't do better to write.

October we all start for Paris where we shall spend this winter and next I suppose. And the only real sad part in all these plans is that I don't see how they will let me go to you in England for even a very short visit. Still I will cling to the last shred of hope and not say no until I am sure that I might not go to Oxford for a short time toward Spring. It is too beautiful a plan to give up dreaming about. At any rate thank you a thousand times for putting the possibility before me.

"And now goodby darling, <u>my</u> darling and please write me very soon. I feel so near you today precious beautiful Louise! I take you in my arms. I kiss your lips, your eyes, your throat. I am,

"Your own own

"<u>Olivia</u>."

"<u>Franzensbad</u>
"Adress Drexel & Harjes."

There is another letter from Franzensbad, this one postmarked September 3, 1893, and on the reverse side of the envelope stamped New York, September 14.

"<u>Franzensbad</u>

"My darling <u>darling</u>,

"Such a love of a letter has just come from you before I have sent off my answer to your last. You are so sweet my beloved. It is your protest against my calling you reserved. In it you say just what I expected you would regarding certain things and thereby confess yourself to be what I thought you—<u>dangerous</u>. Oh no, no your 'sympathy with a nature like Elizabeth's'*is

---

* Probably Elizabeth Ware Winsor, who graduated from Bryn Mawr in 1892, a year before Brownell, and who became the latter's

certainly not going to surprise me! I understood that side of you from the first, the <u>very</u> first. What <u>has</u> surprised me is that, having it, you could feel any love for, or drawing toward me. I have wondered all along if you have seen me as I am. No, your letter doesn't surprise me at all in any particular. Your love for Elizabeth is largely based upon spiritual reverence. You love her first because you honor her. I love you first and last because—<u>I love you</u>, and the honoring and reverencing are quite secondary and subordinate; so much so that if I neither revered nor honored you, I should still love you. Indeed I have loved once, <u>twice</u> where I did not even <u>respect</u>. You see darling, here is where we differ vitally. I am sure I should never dream of requiring that <u>you</u> love without respect. Neither should I for one moment reproach you if for some reason your love for me changed. Of course you must be true to yourself always. This is only a simple statement of facts. My affection for a person is like Desdemona's whose 'love doth so approve him that even his stubborness, his cheeks and frames find favor' with her. The point of all this discourse is that I am confirmed in my fear that perhaps it would not be safe for me to tell you as much about myself as I should like to. How do I know you mightn't break off our relations on the spot? It would be an unspeakable help and blessing to me to feel that whatever I might choose to tell you, you would understand. From the very fact that you are what you are, it would be an unutterable consolation. I do not say approve only understand forgive and not be weaned. But I don't at all know that you <u>could</u> and you might be horrified and

lifelong friend. Around 1900 she married Henry Greenleaf Pearson, who taught English at M.I.T. They had several children.

repelled and that would be fatal. As you say to make a friendship satisfactory there must be a complete frank understanding. This is what I should like but there is a <u>rigorous</u> something about you that frightens me while I admire it. I believe that you are rather <u>implacable</u> <u>inflexible</u> <u>puritanic</u>. Ah me how I love you and how I would like to meet all the requirements of your most rigorous spiritual self.

"If this dear precious unselfish self of yours doesn't see that you've been reserved, why there's nothing to be done. But there is so much, so much in your dear heart and head that I should like to reach. It will surprise you when I declare that no more intimate knowledge of yourself has come to me through your letters than I had by looking in your face the first few times I ever saw you. What I possess of you <u>now</u> I did then. I do not insist that you are responsible for this. It's only another statement of facts.

"Goodby my beloved, my dearly <u>dearly</u> beloved, and don't let the absence or presence of <u>vagueness</u> in this epistle trouble you. Don't answer it at all if it is difficult. Send me another precious letter soon. I kiss you many many times my darling

"Olivia"

And the final letter to Louise Brownell (in any event the final one in the collection of Hamilton College Library), from Fontainebleau, France, no date except Sunday, but with internal evidence (the fact that she and her family were on their way to Étretat on the Normandy coast) indicating it was written in the summer of 1894. An envelope, addressed to Miss Louise S. Brownell, c/o Robert Hode-Bauke, Prager Str. 39, Dresden,

Germany, clarifies the date. It is postmarked Fontainebleau July 30 and on the reverse side is postmarked
Dresden, August 1, 1894. July 30 was a Monday. The
envelope was stamped the day after Olivia wrote the
letter, Sunday, July 29. Clemens was not with his family
at this time. On graduating from Bryn Mawr in 1893,
Louise had been awarded the European Fellowship (the
college's highest honor), consisting of $500 for study in
Europe. In 1893–94 she studied at Oxford and Leipzig
Universities.

"Louise, my darling;

"I don't know how to write you. There seems to be
nothing to say, nothing in all the world, or certainly I
have no adequate language to say anything with. Your
dear letter has come, met me in Paris the other night,
saying you are likely to go to America this year. I was
all unforewarned and it made my heart stand still. I
would not, could not dream this would happen and that
I should lose you now now at the moment of having you
again, after all these years of waiting. It is impossible. I
cannot believe it. It cannot be true. Oh no. Dear dear
Louise, my darling it is too dreadful! I cannot, cannot
bear it! Why didn't you, why couldn't you come to
Étretat? Oh I have lost you and you can do nothing. I
am so miserably helpless. I love you so. I wish you were
here to comfort me. I think I wrote you that we cannot
now afford to live in Hartford and are likely to stay over
here until we can. Do you realise what that may mean?
Another separation like this last,—another interminable
unsatisfied longing to see you. This being apart breaks
breaks my heart. But you will not go. It is a nightmare.
It isn't true. My darling, beloved, this is a naughty in-

considerate letter most discouragingly resembling Marguerite Sweet.—But oh please forgive it and forgive me for I don't ever <u>mean</u> to be a burden to you. But truly this news of yours has so changed the aspect of things made everything look so cruel and hopeless and dark, that I am weak and cowardly tonight, even more so than usual, and the thought of losing you again out of my life seems not [to] be borne at all. It was so dreadful to see you go that morning in London that I feel now almost that I must have had a kind of premonition of this misfortune before us. I love you so much so infinitely, and you are so near and I cannot <u>reach</u> you. Oh if I had known if I had but known I would be in St. Moritz now. But it is too late. Promise me that you will not go away and put the water between us without letting me see you, if you can help it. Promise this one thing my darling and remember that when you are once <u>gone</u>, who can say when we shall be together again? Oh Louise <u>dear</u> Louise don't forget this and <u>let me see you if only to say goodby</u>. If you sail in the Fall try, try to pass through Paris for my sake and let me catch one wee glimpse of you. I implore and beg and beseech you Louise try to do this for me, for if I am to lose you after all I must see you a moment first. Dearest <u>darling</u>, think how important this is to me if it isn't to you. And surely Paris is central and why will it be so hard so impossible for you to leave in that way? Surely you can arrange it I hope and I have written in time for you to try. I must I <u>must</u> see you again! Oh you will not go off without letting me? <u>No no</u> <u>my darling</u>!—I hope very ardently that when you receive this you will drop me a little line letting me know, and giving me an idea of what my fate is to be. Don't keep me waiting to hear from you, for to feel you as near as possible is my greatest blessing and consolation now. It seems I must still keep it well before me that neither separation of time or distance can keep us apart. I believe we have succeeded so far but it is <u>hard</u>. I love you with my whole heart and soul. God bless you for all the good you have brought me and let me keep you always always my own my <u>own</u> inspite of all things.—If you go and I don't see you again for years, I hope it will still be the same with our love. Certainly mine for you can never change. It is fixed and strangely independent of your physical presence, however precious that is.—

"We are spending two or three quiet days here in Fontainebleau on our way to the sea. This is one of those ideal little experiences when everything is so unexpectedly pleasant and lovely. This afternoon we had a long drive through the forest and I did so wish you were with us. In the evening the most beautiful orchestral music drifts in at our windows from somewhere in the darkness back of the trees. But we shall soon be moving on again. I have one more vain proposition to make. At least I'm afraid it's vain. Is there a possibility that you and your sister could shorten your Italian trip a little and come to us in Étretat late in September or early in October perhaps before you sail if you do? Please remember me most cordially to your sister and tell her that we would be delighted if she could come with you. I am glad she will be in Paris next year. I shall see a great deal of her I hope. Oh but the happy happy days I planned to spend with you in that beautiful stimulating great city!—I feel lost without that prospect before me. I must stop. You will let me know that you get all this safely, for if by chance you should not I must

by any chance you should get.
I must repeat all the propositions
requests & lamentations & con-
tours.

Well good night, & God
bless you & make you happy happy
and give you all good things.
Please come in time. And let me
be down in your arms, and
forget everything but the joy of
being near you. — write me
that. You will picture see you

once more little once before
you go. Ah & write soon
& say you love me. Forgive
whatever there is wrong in this
letter. It's my love that's so
violent and unmanning my
poor terrified love that

A page of Susy's final letter to Louise Brownell

Cannot give you up.

Good night darling darling
my beloved — Take you in
my arms & see you Clearly as
you were in London. What a
sacred friendship ours is! —
Ah I long for you so! —
The loneliness the loneliness of
life is the hardest.

Yours for Ever & Ever,

Elma

(No other papers to be found here
This has a disgraceful appearance
Even more so than any other) —

Another page of Susy's letter to Louise Brownell

<u>repeat</u> all the propositions requests and lamentations it contains.

"Well good night, and God bless you and make you happy <u>happy</u> and give you all good things. Please come in to me and let me lie down in your arms, and forget everything but the joy of being near you.—Write me <u>that you will let me see you</u> once, one <u>little</u> once before you go. Oh and write <u>soon</u> and say you love me. Forgive whatever there is wrong in this letter. It's my love that's so violent and demanding my poor terrified love that <u>cannot</u> give you up.

"Good night darling <u>darling</u> my beloved. I take you in my arms and see you clearly as you were in London. What a fated friendship ours is!—Oh I <u>long</u> for you so! —The loneliness the <u>loneliness</u> of life is the hardest.

"Yours for ever and ever

"Olivia

"No other paper to be found here. This has a disgraceful appearance even more so than my others.

"P.S. Oh dear I cannot be brave at all. I am miserably unhappy and full of fear cold terror that I have <u>lost</u> you and that you will <u>go</u> after all go away across the ocean for an endless weary time and I shall not see you before, that you will go without saying goodby. What shall I do if you do? Oh don't <u>don't</u> <u>don't</u> darling darling precious Louise. If I could only go to you!—but you will do all that you can to bring us together won't you? all that you possibly can. I feel wrong and that I am troubling you who are only doing your duty with great sacrifice to yourself. I could not bear to add a feather's weight to your burden dear heart. It's only the thought of the <u>time</u> that we may be held apart when you are gone that makes me feel I <u>must</u> make my request just once when it is all settled even if unfavorably don't be afraid to write me, for I promise to be good and reasonable.

"And now good night my own best beloved. Write soon to your <u>own</u> <u>own</u> Olivia"

What a terrible letter, full of dread, terror, fear of losing Louise, a begging letter written approximately at a time when Clemens was busily writing *Joan of Arc* and reading parts to the idolatrous family (all females), crying at times when he quoted Joan, so strong was his empathy for her (not a good portent of the novel's quality; the novel lacks "distance", humor, is sentimental), and stirring a powerful sympathy for Joan in Susy, Susy who at times was irritated by the name Mark Twain because too often at public functions the attention she received was due, she believed, only to her being the great man's daughter, Susy who now like her father had a persona, a split, and even a sort of pseudonym of her own—at home she was Susy, in the correspondence she was Olivia, and presumably the contents of the letters were kept a secret from all members of her family, although the existence of the correspondence was no secret, the letters from Louise came, Susy's were mailed, and Livy sometimes sent her regards to Louise in Susy's letters. Poor Susy, feeling helpless, useless, her love for Louise (and Louise's for her) had filled her life with meaning, and now the meaning seemed about to abandon her, or had already done so.

She lacked independent means, had no job, no distinct way of life, no way of life of her own, really, and she was helpless to destroy physical distances between herself and Louise. She had dropped out of Bryn Mawr, whereas Louise was doing brilliantly there, had been sent to Europe for further study. Susy had to go where her family went, she was too dependent on her parents —unlike Clara, younger than she, who minded not at all being on her own in Berlin, studying the piano, who as a matter of fact enjoyed the relative personal freedom she had there, and worried her parents, particularly her father, because at times she seemed to ignore or to be unconscious of the Victorian customs which were supposed to circumscribe an unmarried young woman's life, and consequently elicited warnings from him via Livy. It was a difficult, complex time for the Clemenses, and perhaps especially so for the father and his favorite daughter.

How well Susy writes at twenty, twenty-one, twenty-two! How articulate, alive, and mature she is! Questions come to mind. What was happening with Louise? Was she running away from a too-demanding relationship, frightened by Olivia's "violent" (as Susy herself called it) love, perhaps by the physicality of it— what? Are Louise's letters to Olivia extant? It's unlikely that Susy destroyed them. In one of the letters she speaks of keeping them in a trunk. Did the Clemenses discover them after her death? If so, did they destroy them? Before that, did Livy suspect the closeness of the relationship and its great importance to Susy? And did she, after Susy's death, dispose of the letters without letting Clemens know? Were there other letters to Louise which didn't survive, especially any subsequent to the "final" one in the Saunders Papers series? Did Clara, who long outlived her sisters and parents, destroy the letters?

I have inquired about the possible existence of the letters—at the Mark Twain Papers in Berkeley, at the Mark Twain Memorial at Hartford, at the University of Virginia Library, at the Hamilton College Library, and finally at Bryn Mawr, where Louise received a Ph.D. I have struck a cold trail everywhere, even at Bryn Mawr, which in the present year, 1985, is celebrating the 100th anniversary of its founding. The college was born while Susy was writing her biography, and was only half a dozen years old when she matriculated there.

I had hoped at least to find a yearbook photo of Louise at Bryn Mawr, or another Bryn Mawr photo of Olivia (that is, in addition to the one included here and to the variant of it I have seen published elsewhere), or one of Mark Twain taken when he gave the reading, or one of Olivia singing in *Iolanthe,* or a student newspaper's remarks about these events, or some inkling of why Olivia left Bryn Mawr, or a sense of the quality of her classwork there. Leo Dolensky of the college library's manuscript department told me that no student newspaper is extant from those early years of the college's history, that no yearbook is extant, no photo of Louise, no photo of Olivia; that, as a matter of fact, *all* the student records of those years are unaccountably gone, and even the college president's records are missing.

Two last quotations from the letters. In a letter written around the end of March 1893, Susy says, "You see I have come to a conclusion that will utterly shock you, dear, namely that the less we feel the better off we are, and the more good we can do. It's a horrid repulsive conclusion! but really I believe it I think that I live better when I don't feel." What an insight into her emotional state at that time, even if we discount some of it as overly dramatic.

She almost never mentions her father in the letters. (But then on August 29, 1893, he left Europe again for the States, this time staying away from his family for seven months. One wonders about the effect on her of his prolonged absence.) The most prominent mention isn't exactly a flattering one. She made it in a letter from Florence, which I assume from an envelope was postmarked October 1, 1892.

"Papa came home yesterday with his hair <u>shaved</u> tight to his head. You cannot imagine what a sight he is! His poor afflicted family wish he would decline all invitations and withdraw to live the life of a hermit until it grows out again." She doesn't explain why he had his hair shaved. Apparently he had done it on impulse (certainly without warning Susy, who was shocked when she saw him).

Clara Clemens, in her book, *My Father, Mark Twain*, has this to say about the incident. "That morning I was sitting in one of the bedrooms with Susie, when I heard her give a little stifled cry. Turning to look, I observed that she had blushed to the roots of her hair and way down her neck. Following the direction of her eyes, I saw Father standing in the door with his head clipped like a billiard ball. His wonderful hair all gone! No wonder Susie blushed. He looked more like a gatepost than himself. I hated to leave on an absence of several months with this picture in my memory. It has often occurred to me that he must have consented to all this shorn beauty for the fun of seeing horror expressed not only in our faces, but also in the face of the artist who was painting his portrait at the time."

Clemens mentions the event in *The Autobiography of Mark Twain*. "*Sept. 26, '92.*—Arrived in Florence. Got my head shaved. This was a mistake. . . . *Sept. 29, '92.* —I seem able to forget everything except that I have had my head shaved. No matter how closely I shut myself away from draughts it seems to be always breezy up there. But the main difficulty is the flies. They like it up there better than anywhere else; on account of the view, I suppose. It seems to me that I have never seen any flies before that were shod like these. These appear to have talons. Wherever they put their foot down they grab. They walk over my head all the time and cause me infinite torture. It is their park, their club, their summer resort. They have garden parties there and conventions and all sorts of dissipation. And they fear nothing. All flies are daring but these are more daring than those of other nationalities. These cannot be scared away by any device. They are more diligent, too, than the other kinds; they come before daylight and stay till after dark."

The Clemenses embarked for the States in May 1895 after Livy and her children had been abroad continuously for four years. Susy, being the oldest child, had first choice to accompany her parents on Clemens's round-the-world lecture tour to pay off his debts. She declined. In his notebook, mentioned earlier, Clemens states, "We wanted her to go around the world, but she dreaded the sea and elected not to go." So Clara went instead (she left Elmira, New York, with Clemens and Livy in July), and Susy and Jean lived at Quarry Farm

Clemens, Livy, and Clara in Christchurch, New Zealand, November 1895

in Elmira during their parents' extended absence. Susy took up "mental science" in an attempt to steady herself emotionally, and she tried to build up her physical health, her robustness, to add volume to her voice for the time when she intended to resume singing lessons.

Did Susy tell the truth when she claimed fear of the sea as the reason for not going on the great lecture tour? Or was the real reason, possibly, that she wanted to enjoy her freedom (such as it was for a young American bachelor woman in those days) now that she was back in the States, where Louise Brownell was too? She saw Louise again, once in Orange, New Jersey, and in January 1896 (the year of her death) Louise visited her at the farm. Whether they met more often than that I don't

know, nor do I know the nature of their relationship by
now.

A postscript. Louise Sheffield Brownell was born
in 1870 (two years before Susy) and died in 1961 at
ninety-one. In 1889, a year before Susy, she entered
Bryn Mawr. In her freshman year she lived in Radnor
Hall, in her sophomore year in Merion Hall. (Susy had
a room in Radnor Hall.) For a while she was head of
student government. As I have already noted, in 1893–
94 she was at Oxford and Leipzig. In 1894–95 she studied at Barnard College. In 1896–97 she did graduate
work at Bryn Mawr. According to her daughter Silvia,
work on her Ph.D. was finished in 1897 but the degree
was not granted and sent to her until 1954, when the
requirements were reduced. In 1897 she was appointed
warden of Sage College, the women's part of Cornell
University. She taught English literature at Cornell.
She met Arthur Percy Saunders in the fall of 1899 when
he came to Cornell as an Honorary Fellow in the Chemistry Department. They were engaged late in January.
In May he was hired to teach chemistry at Hamilton
College, a small college for men. She married Saunders
August 30, 1900, at age thirty. She had four children:
Silvia (1901–); Olivia (named after Olivia Clemens;
Olivia was married to the writer James Agee 1933–38;
later she married Robert W. Wood, Jr., and lived in
Princeton) (1904–); William Duncan (1904–1922), who
died as the result of an accident at Hamilton College;
and Percy Blake (1911–).

A postpostscript. According to Silvia Saunders,
Jesse Benedict Carter (1872–1917) of Princeton was a
"close friend of Louise's in Europe in 1893 and afterwards. Some of Louise's friends were critical of this re-

Louise Brownell at thirty

lationship." I don't know why they were critical, nor do I know the nature of the relationship. I wonder if Susy knew of this friendship, and if so, if she was jealous of it.

Still another note. If Clemens felt threatened, as apparently he did, by Susy's growing love for Bryn Mawr, it could not have been reassuring to hear her college friends call her by another name than the one used at home—Olivia, which was also his wife's name. (Shades of the Electra complex!—this must at least have aroused confusion in Clemens.) Susy's decision to use her first name on this, her major break from home, probably stimulated his sense of the psychological distance she was putting between herself and home (and him), a distance highlighted by her embarrassment over his telling of the ghost story, a favorite of his. His telling it despite the promise may have been his way of asserting his identity and the old hierarchical relationship between them. She was on dubious ground in asking for the promise, for she was asserting her claims on him at the very time she was distancing herself. From the new height of her collegiate sophistication, she was being judgmental about his material. As it turned out, he knew his audience (and himself) better than she did. In any event, he was right to be himself. His mistake was to grant the promise. Hers was to forget she was dealing, after all, with a genius, whose temperamental sides she was not unacquainted with.

Long, long ago, when I had a friendship with the great German novelist Thomas Mann, one of his daughters returned to New York, where I was living, after a visit to her parents in Southern California. When I asked how it had gone, she made an unhappy face.

"Your mother?" I inquired, knowing her mother to be a strong, sometimes dominating woman. "No," she replied to my surprise. "My father uses up all the oxygen in the house." Clemens too must have been using up a great deal of it, causing Susy to enjoy the fresh air of Bryn Mawr.

As for Louise Brownell's first name: it was also Susy's mother's middle name. But although I include this detail for the record, I'm not at all sure there's much, if any, significance in it.

Did Clemens know Louise Brownell Saunders or about her? Yes. Two letters from him to her have survived and are among the Saunders family papers at Hamilton College. I have been unable to locate the letters which elicited his replies. His first letter is dated "New York, Sept. 3." Its envelope, postmarked Deal-beach, N.J., September 3, 1904, is addressed in his hand to "Mrs. A. P. Saunders, Clinton, N.Y." On it is written, in another hand (probably Mrs. Saunders's), "Mr. Clemens—for Olivia." Presumably Mrs. Saunders was saving the letter for her daughter, who at the time of Clemens's response was a day short of four months old (Olivia Saunders was born on May 4, 1904). The year 1904 had been a hard one for Clemens. His wife, Livy, had died in Florence on June 5.

"Dear Mrs. Saunders:
"I am grateful to have those hallowed names thus consecrated, and in reverence I bow my white head before them in their new place. How long they stood for the grace and beauty and joy of life—and now, how they stand for measureless pain and loss!

"We are come upon evil days: may they be few!
"Affectionately
                              "S. L. Clemens"

From this letter (as well as from the second, as we shall see) we can infer that Mrs. Saunders had informed Clemens that she had named her second daughter after Olivia Susan Clemens. But what did he mean by "those hallowed names"? Why the plural form? Puzzled, I phoned Mrs. Olivia Wood, who had been named after Susy and with whom I had previously spoken. Was her middle name Susan? No, she replied. She said she was sure she had been christened Olivia but she wasn't sure if she had a middle name. She thought she *may* have been christened Clemens as a middle name but wasn't certain. However, she had been called, and she had called herself, Olivia Clemens Saunders at least from the time she was ten. On further thought, she said that very possibly she *had* been christened Clemens. So probably Clemens had used the plural form because he was referring to two names: Olivia Clemens.

Regardless of whether Mrs. Saunders had intended to memorialize two persons (Olivia Susan Clemens and Olivia Louise Clemens) by naming her child Olivia Clemens, the double allusion must have been as powerful as it was inevitable for Clemens, who was still trying to digest and adjust to the dreadful loss of Livy. It is this which he feels when he writes, "How long they stood for the grace and beauty and joy of life" and "We are come upon evil days: may they be few!" It is likely that Mrs. Saunders had learned about Livy's death before she wrote to Clemens. Clemens seems to know that she shares this knowledge. His brief letter resonates with the double loss. But could Mrs. Saunders—except as an afterthought—have intended a double memorial? No— her child had been born a month before Livy's death.

The second letter, written on stationery imprinted "Dublin, New Hampshire," is dated "Oct. 16/06." Its envelope is postmarked Dublin. Addressed in Clemens's hand to "Mrs. Louise Brownell Saunders, Clinton, N.Y.," it notes, also in his hand, that it is "From S. L. Clemens, 21 Fifth Ave., New York."

"Dear Mrs. Saunders:

"Your moving letter has reached me—and my heart —and finds a grateful welcome. It is a deep pleasure to me to know that you think I am writing worthily of Susy and her mother—that beautiful and inspiring and pathetic theme. So rare they were! I think they left not many of their lofty rank in the world when they quitted it. I wish, with you, that Livy could have known that your child was to bear Susy's name and keep her dear memory green in your heart.

"I thank you, *thank* you, for your letter.

"With my love—S. L. Clemens"

What did Clemens have in mind when he wrote, "It is a deep pleasure to me to know that you think I am writing worthily of Susy and her mother . . ."? My guess is that Mrs. Saunders had referred specifically to one of the three excerpts of Clemens's autobiography which had appeared in the *North American Review* that year. An examination of the periodical for 1906 shows that the publication of the first of the twenty-five installments of the autobiography mentioned earlier (they continued into 1907) began in the issue of September 7.

The installments were titled "Chapters from My Autobiography." A note by the editor of the review informed the reader that no part of the autobiography would appear in book form during the author's lifetime. In the first excerpt Clemens wrote about his ancestors, his parents, his brother Orion and sister Pamela, and about James Lampton, his mother's favorite cousin and the model for Colonel Sellers of his first novel, *The Gilded Age*, which he co-authored with Charles Dudley Warner. He mentioned neither Susy nor her biography of him. In the second excerpt (September 21) he discussed his early experiences as an author, offered an anecdote about his youth in Hannibal, Missouri, and recalled a meeting with Robert Louis Stevenson in Washington Square, New York. Again he didn't allude to Susy or her biography.

However, in the third installment (October 5), he wrote about Livy, Susy's death, the terrific impact of it on him, and reminisced at length about Susy's childhood. It is this excerpt to which Mrs. Saunders had probably referred. True, the fourth installment (October 19) contained many comments about Susy as well as parts of her biography. Also true, I don't know when it became available to subscribers and other customers. But it seems unlikely that Mrs. Saunders had access to it sufficiently prior to October 19 for her to write to Clemens about it and for him to reply on October 16, the date of his second letter.

Aside from its intrinsic merits as a fine though brief communication by Clemens, the letter is interesting in at least three respects. It shows conclusively he knew that Mrs. Saunders had named her second daugh-

ter in memory of his beloved Susy; that he politely ignored her naming her daughter as Olivia rather than as
Susy (he accepts, however courteously, no Olivia in his
reply—we recall his probably mixed emotions when at
Bryn Mawr he heard Susy called Olivia, his wife's
name); and that he was informal enough with Mrs.
Saunders to refer to his wife not as Mrs. Clemens, as
was often his way with correspondents, but as Livy.
That Mrs. Saunders had touched his heart is witnessed
not only by his saying as much but also by his signing
the letter "With my love." Had Mrs. Saunders managed, even if unconsciously, even if only fleetingly, to
fill some of the aching void in Clemens's heart caused
by Susy's untimely death, to fill it because she had been
close to Susy, close enough to name her daughter in her
memory, close enough to be now a kind of daughter
surrogate for Clemens?

Given his strong feelings about Bryn Mawr, feelings which suggest jealousy, it is hard for me to believe
he would be so cordial to Mrs. Saunders if he had
known the nature of the correspondence between her
and Susy, or at any rate (judging by Susy's epistolary
responses to Louise Brownell) if he had read Louise's
side of it, the only one to which he might have had
access. I wonder why Mrs. Saunders's letters to him
dealing with Susy haven't survived, whereas a letter to
him by her, dated Clinton, N.Y., May 14, 1905, asking
him to inscribe a copy of *Joan of Arc* for a friend, is still
extant in the Mark Twain Papers in Berkeley. Can the
same person or persons who were responsible for the
presumed suppression or destruction of Louise Brownell's letters to Susy also have suppressed or destroyed
Mrs. Saunders's Susy-related letters to Clemens?

During the summer of 1896 Clemens, Livy, and
Clara were still abroad, having completed his round-
the-world lecture tour. He was in his sixty-first year.
Katy Leary, the long-time Clemens maid, noticed an
odd change in Susy, who was visiting in Hartford. Susy
seemed unusually restless, and in strange, ambiguous
ways unlike herself. Her health, Katy Leary thought,
was failing. The doctor who was called said Susy was
suffering from overwork and needed isolation and rest.
But although Susy rested she did not get better, so her
aunt in Elmira was sent for, and Joseph Twichell, a
Hartford pastor who was a dear friend of Clemens,
came down to Hartford from a summer place in the
Adirondacks.

On August 15 the doctor diagnosed Susy's illness as
spinal meningitis. That evening she ate for the last time.
Next morning, a Sunday, she walked about a bit in pain
and delirium, then felt very weak and returned to bed,
but before doing so, rummaging in a closet, she came
across a gown she had once seen her mother wear. She
thought the gown was her dead mother and, kissing it,
began to cry.

Dixon Wecter, in *The Love Letters of Mark Twain*
(1949) wrote, ". . . she paced the floor in a raging fever,
often taking pen and paper to scribble . . . notes in a
large sometimes incoherent hand. . . . She fancied that
her companion was La Malibran, famous Parisian
mezzo-soprano who had died sixty years before, at only
little more than Susy's age—after days of terrible suffering from an accident in which she had been thrown by
a horse." Then he quoted 113 words of the scribbles.

I shall quote them in their entirety. They are about
1,000 words long. In the manuscript they appear on

forty-seven sheets of 9″ × 5³/4″ lined paper on which she wrote against the lines. The script is large, as if she's having trouble seeing, and it's flowing: the words often run together. The writing is on one side of the paper. The pages are not numbered. Their order is not immutable. To some extent I have put them together with my own sense of their order. Some of the pages may not have survived.

"[You?] will be held by and obey me in order that you can hold & command the world. Say I will try not to doubt and I *will* obey my benefactress Mme. Malibran Now I can better hold you. You must not deliberately question me & my wisdom while I am only making the destiny which you feel in your heart possible. I do not allow such treatment   Say 'I will obey Mme Malibran' 'I freely decide to obey Mme. Malibran.' Now go and *hold* this song. Nothing but indecision Go on Go on Yes does she bow her too white head? She must she must she must Yes my black Princess. You and Miss Two will meet on equal terms & on dissimalal ground in future You are her superior in strength & power and intellectual courage She is yours in purity and character and peace   Still you are not bad in character but good Your evolution is greater momentarily along other lines   never mind she will not despise the full flower of your spirit   No but I mean she will say I can learn of her even in this my own proper province and in the others where where is she? Tell her to kiss you and say I am sure you are safe and on the whole best guided by your equal and superior Mme. Maria Felicia Malibran Tell her to say you shall express it magnificent darkness of the Lord. Tell her to say I am convinced that you and Mrs Warner are helpful to each other   Tell her to say—God bless the shadows as I bless the light   Tell her to say, I am pure & free & good and peaceful & charitable & lovely and gracious & clear sighted but too that I am still *weak*   In strength I bow to Mme. Malibran Mr. Clemens Mr. Zola Mr. Wait   She must endorse it. There is no appeal from my command & statetus [statutes?] of the inexorable Lord. She is not unjust. Love governs all thereby. Let her admit that even her innate purity and perfection of c a [character?] inclines her to dread for you the temptations of the world   She cannot save you from them but I can make you overcome them   It is from the earth that you & I do get our size and force and dominance and for the earth we use these gifts. She is the last person to deny the law of compensation   Yes I am anxious that she who rules by peace & purity & love of God should concede to me the dominance of those great things which the earth gives forth to man and God   I want her to bow to me & say I see that even darkness can be great, that even passion can be power converted into power that even tragedy is mine & hers & God's in his great infallible and never changing law. She has not understood these things. Light is her own but darkn[ess] she dispells   In me darkness must remain from everlasting to everlasting forever sometimes less painful darkness but darkness is the complement of light yes tell her to say she trusts you child of great darkness and light to me who can keep the darkness universal and free from sensual taint and lead her on to strength & power & peace. Let her say she believes that you and Mrs. Warner of the great musical power & mastery can under my auspices do each other nothing but *good*. Let

her say more that darkness is not bad but good not monstrous but beautiful that I stand as high in my destiny as
she stands in hers. She is a queen of God's light but I am
a queen of his darkness. You will never follow far
enough in her footsteps artistically to dominate the ar-
tistic world with light. wuld exclude you therefore from
all dominance? This is the arrogance which the Lord
alone may hold. Let her say I am convinced that what
must be is and my tenderness and suffering & sympathy
with the world of suffering shall not blind me even momentarily to the eternal truths. Let her say that you
shall write tragedy sing tragedy utter tragedy & she will
listen without pain or flinching   Rosco Darcey has [il-
legible] her I wrote it is absurd. She did not want to
hear about the wounded dog & the worse wounded
man   She must give ear to these things not reluctantly
but gladly as we do   In time so will Miss Davis, so will
Mrs. Allen so will Mrs. Walker so will Mrs Tuller. They
have been seeking God's light & shunning his darkness
They will inherit the greater darkness to come for this
is retribution not vengeance Rosco Darcey is true it is a
fact   You cannot get away from it   God will not allow
it. You cannot escape his creations. The Universe is
united   *You* may not dissever greatnesses of the earth.
Greatness has no need of shunning. Melody a sin is not
of God. But [illegible: eternity?] my God let us revere
it   let her face it let her contemplate it. Weakness she
has why not? Who ever got strength from the heavens? I
cannot have her dissever from your future as imperson-
ated in the gifted and great body of Mrs. Charles Dudley Warner without experiencing a sense of pain and
displeasure   Yes she must not falter in her decision of
holding you to accomplish this end which *I* direct   She

sees and understands that I am come to bring su[ccor?] to your ills. And she does not really question my great vision I am perfectly convinced that you and *Mrs Warner* are *fundamentally & essentially* congenial and *I insist* in my capacity as principal directress of your future and your fate that you* have no one [illegible: stray?] from her [illegible: art?] stay stay stay Mr Dickens Mr Balzac Mr Lowell Mr Osborn Mrs Warner and Olivia Langdon Clemens"

It was these scraps and scribbles that Clemens referred to when he wrote to Livy from England at 6 P.M. of August 19, the day after Susy's death. He had been informed of her death by cable. Livy and Clara were still on the steamer, heading for New York and the tragic news that would greet them on arrival.

"I have spent the day alone—thinking; sometimes bitter thoughts, sometimes only sad ones. . . . Reproaching myself for a million things whereby I have brought misfortune and sorrow to this family. And I have been re-reading Sue's letter [Susan Crane] received day before yesterday, and written three days and a half after Susy's attack of mania; for I read it with a new light now and perceive that it has warnings in it that were not before apparent. Yes, and I have been searching for letters—fruitlessly. I have no letter that Susy wrote me—oh, not so much as a line. Sue says that in our house after they took her there she was up and dressed and writing all the time—poor troubled head! I hope they have kept every scrap; for they must often have suspected that these were the last things that would flow from that subtle brain. I know that if they

* The next seven words are scratched over in the manuscript.

are there you will find them. I wish she had written something to me—but I did not deserve it. You did, but I did not. You always wrote her, over-burdened with labors as you were—you the most faithful, the most loyal wife, mother, friend in the earth—but I neglected her as I neglect everybody in my selfishness. Everybody but you. I have always written to you; for you are always in my heart, always in my mind. . . ."

At about noon that Sunday of August 18 Susy became blind. "I am blind, Uncle Charlie, and you are blind," she said to her uncle, who was at her bedside. But she was confused. It was not Uncle Charlie, but rather Uncle Theodore [Crane]. She spoke for the last time about an hour later when, groping with her hands and finding Katy Leary, she caressed Katy's face and said, "Mama." A little later she fell into a coma and remained unconscious until the evening of Tuesday, the 18th, when she died. She was twenty-four years and five months old.

As we saw, Dixon Wecter wrote that Susy "fancied that her companion was La Malibran." But there are many voices in the delirium notes, and sometimes Susy is addressing herself, having a dialogue with herself. In a delirium, who can tell what allusions are streaming where? Is Susy also Mme. Malibran? Is Malibran also Marchesi, Susy's singing teacher in Paris? Does Malibran suggest Caliban, the dark figure in Shakespeare's *The Tempest?* Does Miss Two imply Miss Double, or Miss Two-Faced? Is "my black Princess" a suggestion of the Prince of Darkness? Is Rosco Darcey also the Fitzgerald Darcy of *Pride and Prejudice?* Is Mrs. Warner also Mrs. Warn-Her?

Because of her prominence in the delirium notes let

me offer some details of Malibran's dramatic life. She
was a contralto with a high soprano register, and famous for her fiery, restless, feverish, magnetic temperament. She was celebrated for her Desdemona (Rossini)
and her Norma. She was born in Paris on March 24,
1808, the daughter of Manuel García, a famous Spanish
tenor, with whom she studied. He was notoriously
harsh and overbearing with her. She was the elder sister
of Pauline Viardot, another famous mezzo-soprano.

She made her opera debut in London in June 1825
as Rosina in *The Barber of Seville*. She was a great success
there, on the Continent, and in New York, where she
sang with her father's opera company in 1825–26 in Mo-
zart, Rossini, and in two operas written especially for
her by her father. In an effort to escape her father's
tyrannical presence, she married a French-American
merchant, François Eugène Malibran, in New York, but
was unhappy with him and soon left him. In 1827 she
sang in Grace Church and on the Bowery in New York.

She returned to Europe alone that year and had
great triumphs singing in Paris, London, Rome, Milan,
and Naples. In 1830 she fell in love with Charles de
Bériot, a Belgian concert violinist, and lived openly
with him. Succeeding in having her marriage annulled,
she married de Bériot late in March 1836. In London in
April she was thrown by a horse while she was preg-
nant, receiving a bad head injury. Although unwell, she
insisted on singing in the Manchester Festival in September. She died September 23, 1836, in Manchester,
nine days after her last appearance and six months after
her second marriage. Alfred de Musset wrote a poem,
"Stances," as a tribute to her a fortnight after her death.

Susy may have felt she had several key things in

common with her: a desire to be an opera star (realized so brilliantly in Malibran's case); being temperamental, passionate; being the daughter of a famous father; being the eldest daughter; and, if she sensed the imminence of her death, dying tragically young (Malibran was twenty-eight at her death). She may also have felt she had an overbearing father. Malibran was sexual; she lived openly with de Bériot. Whether Susy was ever overtly sexual I don't know.

Before proceeding to a brief discussion of the delirium notes, it seems to me worth noting that they stand as further witness to the remarkable qualities of Susy's mind, which her father so admired. They are beautiful and moving, and show that even as she was dying, her mind was very active and noble.

The many allusions aside, the delirium notes replay —on a brilliantly lighted stage, in a feverish but remarkably articulate manner, and with great complexity of voices—the leading motifs of the letters to Louise Brownell: the two sides of the antithesis: the queen of God's light against the queen of his darkness; spirituality versus earthiness. (Susy's love of and understanding of Wagner may have played a part here.) And, as in the letters, Susy is cast as the earthy, passionate, unreserved one—at least great friend if not lover. Understandably, in her dying hours she heard many voices that justified her. As for the importance of Mrs. Warner in the notes, her first name was Susy, she was a leading figure in Hartford's musical life, and during Livy's long absence abroad she very probably served as a stand-in mother for Susy.

Clemens wrote in his autobiography, "The last thirteen days of Susy's life were spent in our own house in Hartford, the home of her childhood and always the dearest place in the earth to her. About her she had faithful old friends—her pastor, Mr. Twichell, who had known her from her cradle and who had come a long journey to be with her; her uncle and aunt, Mr. and Mrs. Theodore Crane; Patrick, the coachman; Katy, who had begun to serve us when Susy was a child of eight years; John and Ellen, who had been with us many years. Also Jean was there." Jean was Susy's youngest sister.

Of Susy's last word, "Mama," he wrote, "How gracious it was that in that forlorn hour of wreck and ruin, with the night of death closing around her, she should have been granted that beautiful illusion—that the latest vision which rested upon the clouded mirror of her mind should have been the vision of her mother, and the latest emotion she should know in life the joy and peace of that dear imagined presence."

In *Mark Twain's Notebook* Paine stated, "In the burning heat of those final days in Hartford she would walk to the window or lie on the couch in her fever and delirium, and when the cars went by would say: 'Up go the trolley cars for Mark Twain's daughter. Down go the trolley cars for Mark Twain's daughter.' This was no more than a day or two before the end."

Clemens, with Livy and Clara, sailed on the *Norman* from Capetown in mid-July, a year almost to the day since they had left Elmira. He had high hopes now of paying off all his debts dollar for dollar instead of the fifty cents on the dollar he had agreed upon with his creditors. And he looked forward to beginning work soon on his new travel book in England. The Clemenses arrived in Southampton on the 31st and proceeded to rent a house in Guildford, where they expected to await the arrival of Susy, Jean, and Katy Leary no later than August 12.

At first no news came. Then, on Friday the 14th, there was a letter saying that Susy was slightly ill—nothing to worry about. But the Clemenses, upset, cabled for later news. All that Friday there was no answer. A ship was due to leave from Southampton for New York next day at noon. Livy and Clara began to pack in order to be ready to depart in case bad news should come. Finally there was a cable, saying, "Wait for cablegram in the morning."

This was not in the least reassuring. Clemens cabled again and asked that the reply be sent to Southampton. That night, in the hope that good news would still come, he waited in the local post office until the place closed around midnight. Still no further message.

Clemens wrote in his autobiography:

"We sat silent at home till one in the morning, waiting—waiting for we knew not what. Then we took the earliest morning train and when we reached Southampton the message was there. It said the recovery would be long but certain. This was a great relief to me but not to my wife. She was frightened. She and Clara went aboard the steamer at once and sailed for America to nurse Susy. I remained behind to search for another and larger house in Guildford.

"That was the 15th of August, 1896. Three days later, when my wife and Clara were about halfway across the ocean, I was standing in our dining room, thinking of nothing in particular, when a cablegram was put into my hand. It said, 'Susy was peacefully released today.'

"It is one of the mysteries of our nature that a man,

all unprepared, can receive a thunder-stroke like that
and live. There is but one reasonable explanation of it.
The intellect is stunned by the shock and but gropingly
gathers the meaning of the words. The power to realize
their full import is mercifully wanting. The mind has a
dumb sense of vast loss—that is all. . . ."

How many times have I read Clemens's account of
the immense shock the news of Susy's death was for
him. Yet now, in reading him yet again, I'm profoundly
saddened—and amazed by his ability to express in language (and so soon after a tragic personal event) all his
feelings, and in a way I can only think of as sublime. On
the occasion of each of the monstrous blows that struck
him, he almost immediately set down on paper his
thoughts and deepest emotions—and often his sense of
his own great guilt. He wrote a terrible letter on the
death of his brother Henry, who, as we recall, was
killed in the explosion of the *Pennsylvania*, blaming himself for that death, and wrote very soon after the deaths
of Livy and Jean. Perhaps I'm particularly moved because my own daughter's name is Susy, the spelling of
which was modelled on that of Susy Clemens.

Clemens continued:

"The 18th of August brought me the awful tidings.
The mother and the sister were out there in mid-Atlan-
tic, ignorant of what was happening, flying to meet this
incredible calamity. All that could be done to protect
them from the full force of the shock was done by rela-
tives and good friends. They went down the Bay and
met the ship at night but did not show themselves until
morning and then only to Clara. When she returned to
the stateroom she did not speak and did not need to.
Her mother looked at her and said, 'Susy is dead.'

"At half past ten o'clock that night Clara and her

mother completed their circuit of the globe and drew up at Elmira by the same train and in the same car which had borne them and me westward from it one year, one month and one week before. And again Susy was there—not waving her welcome in the glare of the lights as she had waved her farewell to us thirteen months before, but lying white and fair in her coffin in the house where she was born. . . .

"On the 23rd her mother and her sisters saw her laid to rest—she that had been our wonder and our worship."

The New York *Times* of Sunday, August 23, carried the following item: "LEARNS OF HER DAUGHTER'S DEATH/ Mrs. Clemens Faints When the News Is Broken to Her.

"Among the passengers who arrived yesterday on the American Line Steamship Paris were the wife and daughter of Samuel L. Clemens (Mark Twain), whose eldest daughter, Olivia Susan Clemens, died on Tuesday night last, at the home in Hartford, Conn.

"Mr. Clemens, who was expected also, had started, with his wife and Miss Clara, the second daughter, when news of their eldest daughter's illness reached them, but was detained on business at the last moment in Southampton. He, therefore, was advised of the death by cable while Mrs. Clemens and the sister were on the ocean.

"They were notified by Dr. [Clarence C.] Rice [a New York physician], a friend of the family, who boarded the Paris at Quarantine. The mother was prostrated and swooned when the news was conveyed to her.

"A carriage awaited the party at the pier, and they went directly to the Grand Central Station.

"Mr. Clemens sailed from Southampton yesterday for New-York."

This last bit of information was in error, as perhaps also the note about Livy's swooning.

On September 27 Clemens wrote from London to Twichell in Hartford.

"Through Livy and Katy I have learned, dear old Joe, how loyally you stood poor Susy's friend and mine and Livy's. How you came all the way down twice from your summer refuge on your merciful errands to bring the peace and comfort of your beloved presence, first to that poor child and again to the broken heart of her poor desolate mother. It was like you, like your good great heart, like your matchless and unmatchable self.

"It was no surprise to me to learn that you stayed by Susy long hours, careless of fatigue and heat. It was no surprise to me to learn that you could still the storms that swept her spirit when no other could, for she loved you, revered you, trusted you, and 'Uncle Joe' was no empty phrase upon her lips.

"I am grateful to you, Joe, grateful to the bottom of my heart, which has always been filled with love for you, and respect and admiration. And I would have chosen you out of all the world to take my place at Susy's side and Livy's in those black hours.

"Susy was a rare creature, the rarest that has been reared in Hartford in this generation. And Livy knew it, and you knew it, and Charley Warner and George, and Harmony, and the Hillyers and the Dunhams and the Cheneys, and Susy and Lilly, and the Bunces, and Henry Robinson and Dick Burton, and perhaps others. And I also was of the number but not in the same degree, for she was above my duller comprehension. I merely knew that she was my superior in fineness of mind, in the delicacy and subtlety of her intellect. But to fully measure her I was not competent.

"I know her better now, for I have read her private writings and sounded the deeps of her mind. And I know better now the treasure that was mine than I knew it when I had it. But I have this consolation: that dull as I was, I always knew enough to be proud when she commended me or my work—as proud as if Livy had done it herself—and I took it as the accolade from the hand of genius. I see now, as Livy always saw, that she had greatness in her and that she herself was dimly conscious of it.

"And now she is dead—and I can never tell her.

"God bless you Joe—and all of your house."

The following day Clemens wrote to Henry C. Robinson in Hartford.

"It is as you say, dear old friend, 'the pathos of it.' . . . All the circumstances of this death were pathetic. My brain is worn to rags rehearsing them. The mere death would have been cruelty enough, without over-loading it and emphasizing it with that score of harsh and wanton details. The child was taken away when her mother was within three days of her, and would have given three decades for the sight of her.

"In my despair and unassuageable misery I upbraid myself for ever parting with her. But there is no use in that. Since it was to happen, it would have happened."

On January 19, 1897, still in London, Clemens wrote to Twichell.

"Do I want you to write to me? Indeed I do. I do not want most people to write but I do want you to do it. The others break my heart but you will not. You have a something divine in you that is not in other men. You have the touch that heals, not lacerates. And you know the secret places of our hearts. You know our life —the outside of it—as the others do—and the inside of it—which they do not. You have seen our whole voyage. You have seen us go to sea, a cloud of sail, and the flag at the peak. And you see us now, chartless, adrift—derelicts, battered, water-logged, our sails a ruck of rags, our pride gone. For it is gone. And there is nothing in its place. The vanity of life was all we had, and there is no more vanity left in us. We are even ashamed of that we had, ashamed that we trusted the promises of life and builded high—to come to this!

"I did not know that Susy was part of us. I did *not* know that she could go away. I did not know that she could go away and take our lives with her, yet leave our dull bodies behind. And I did not know what she was. To me she was but treasure in the bank, the amount known, the need to look at it daily, handle it, weigh it, count it, *realize* it, not necessary. And now that I would do it, it is too late. They tell me it is not there, has vanished away in a night, the bank is broken, my fortune is gone, I am a pauper. How am I to comprehend this? How am I to *have* it? Why am I robbed, and who is benefited?

"Ah well, Susy died at *home*. She had that privilege. Her dying eyes rested upon nothing that was strange to them, but only upon things which they had known and loved always and which had made her young years glad. And she had you and Sue and Katy and John and Ellen. This was happy fortune. I am thankful that it was vouchsafed to her. If she had died in another house— well, I think I could not have borne that. To us, our house was not unsentient matter. It had a heart and a soul and eyes to see us with and approvals and solicitudes and deep sympathies. It was of us and we were in its confidence and lived in its grace and in the peace of its benediction. We never came home from an absence that its face did not light up and speak out its eloquent welcome. And we could not enter it unmoved. And could we now, oh now, in spirit we should enter it unshod.

"I am trying to add to the 'assets' which you estimate so generously. No, I am not. The thought is not in my mind. My purpose is other. I am working but it is for the sake of the work—the 'surcease of sorrow' that is found there. I work all the days, and trouble vanishes away when I use that magic. This book *[Following the Equator]* will not long stand between it and me now. But that is no matter, I have many unwritten books to fly to for my preservation. The interval between the finishing of this one and the beginning of the next will not be more than an hour, at most. *Continuances*, I mean, for two of them are already well along. In fact I have reached exactly the same stage in their journey: 19,000 words each. The present one will contain 180,000 words —130,000 are done. I am well protected. . . .

"Some day you and I will walk again, Joe, and talk. I hope so. We could have *such* talks! We are all grateful to you and Harmony—*how* grateful it is not given to us to say in words. We pay as we can, in love, and in this coin practicing no economy. Goodbye, dear old Joe!"

On Susy's gravestone in Elmira is carved the following:

OLIVIA SUSAN CLEMENS
MAR. 19, 1872—AUG. 18, 1896

"WARM SUMMER SUN
　　SHINÉ KINDLY HERE
WARM SOUTHERN WIND
　　BLOW SOFTLY HERE
GREEN SOD ABOVE
　　LIE LIGHT, LIE LIGHT—
GOOD NIGHT, DEAR HEART,
　　GOOD NIGHT, GOOD NIGHT"
　　ROBERT RICHARDSON

A year after her death Clemens wrote a poem in her memory, which was published in the November 1897 issue of *Harper's Magazine*. I reprint it not for its strength as poetry (Clemens was no poet) but as a testimonial to the strength of his attachment to Susy.

IN MEMORIAM.
OLIVIA SUSAN CLEMENS.
DIED AUGUST 18, 1896; AGED 24.

In a fair valley—oh, how long ago, how long ago!—
Where all the broad expanse was clothed in vines
And fruitful fields and meadows starred with flowers,
And clear streams wandered at their idle will,
And still lakes slept, their burnished surfaces
A dream of painted clouds, and soft airs
Went whispering with odorous breath,
And all was peace—in that fair vale,
Shut from the troubled world, a nameless hamlet
　　drowsed.
　　Hard by, apart, a temple stood;

And strangers from the outer world
Passing, noted it with tired eyes,
And seeing, saw it not:
A glimpse of its fair form—an answering momentary
    thrill—
And they passed on, careless and unaware.

They could not know the cunning of its make;
They could not know the secret shut up in its heart;
Only the dwellers of the hamlet knew:
They knew that what seemed brass was gold;
What marble seemed, was ivory;
The glories that enriched the milky surfaces—
The trailing vines, and interwoven flowers,
And tropic birds awing, clothed all in tinted fire—
They knew for what they were, not what they
    seemed:
Encrustings all of gems, not perishable splendors of
    the brush.
They knew the secret spot where one must stand—
They knew the surest hour, the proper slant of sun—
To gather in, unmarred, undimmed,
The vision of the fane in all its fairy grace,
A fainting dream against the opal sky.
        And more than this. They knew
That in the temple's inmost place a spirit dwelt,
Made all of light!
        For glimpses of it they had caught
Beyond the curtains when the priests
That served the altar came and went.

        All loved that light and held it dear
That had this partial grace;

But the adoring priests alone who lived
By day and night submerged in its immortal glow
Knew all its power and depth, and could appraise the
    loss
If it should fade and fail and come no more.

    All this was long ago—so long ago!

The light burned on; and they that worship'd it,
And they that caught its flash at intervals and held it
    dear,
Contented lived in its secure possession. Ah,
How long ago it was!
                    And then when they
Were nothing fearing, and God's peace was in the air,
And none was prophesying harm—
The vast disaster fell:
Where stood the temple when the sun went down,
Was vacant desert when it rose again!
    Ah, yes! 'Tis ages since it chanced!

                    So long ago it was,
That from the memory of the hamlet-folk the Light
    has passed—
They scarce believing, now, that once it was,
Or if believing, yet not missing it,
And reconciled to have it gone.

    Not so the priests! Oh, not so
The stricken ones that served it day and night,
Adoring it, abiding in the healing of its peace:
They stand, yet, where erst they stood
Speechless in that dim morning long ago;
And still they gaze, as then they gazed,

And murmur, "It will come again;
It knows our pain—it knows—it knows—
Ah, surely it will come again."

S.L.C.

Lake Lucerne, August 18, 1897

Santa Cruz, California
May 8, 1985

Foreword

by Mark Twain

Susy was born the 19th of March, 1872. The summer seasons of her childhood were spent at Quarry Farm on the hills east of Elmira, New York; the other seasons of the year at the home in Hartford. (We removed to Hartford in October 1871 and presently built a house.) Like other children, she was blithe and happy, fond of play; *un*like the average of children, she was at times much given to retiring within herself and trying to search out the hidden meanings of the deep things that make the puzzle and pathos of human existence and in all the ages have baffled the inquirer and mocked him. As a little child aged seven she was oppressed and perplexed by the maddening repetition of the stock incidents of our race's fleeting sojourn here, just as the same thing has oppressed and perplexed maturer minds from the beginning of time. A myriad of men are born; they labor and sweat and struggle for bread; they squabble and scold and fight; they scramble for little mean advantages over each other. Age creeps upon them; infirmities follow; shames and humiliations bring down their prides and their vanities. Those they love are taken from them and the joy of life is turned to aching grief. The burden of pain, care, misery, grows heavier year by year. At length ambition is dead; pride is dead; vanity is dead; longing for release is in their place. It comes at last—the only unpoisoned gift earth ever had for them—and they vanish from a world where they were of no consequence; where they achieved nothing; where they were a mistake and a failure and a foolishness; where they have left no sign that they have existed—a world which will lament them a day and forget them forever. Then another myriad takes their place and copies all they did and goes along the same profitless road and vanishes as they vanished—to make room for another and another and a million other myriads to follow the same arid path through the same desert and accomplish what the first myriad and all the myriads that came after it accomplished—nothing!

"Mamma, what is it all for?" asked Susy, preliminarily stating the above details in her own halting language, after long brooding over them alone in the privacy of the nursery.

A year later she was groping her way alone through another sunless bog, but this time she reached a rest for her feet. For a week, her mother had not been able to go to the nursery, evenings, at the child's prayer hour. She spoke of it—was sorry for it and said she would come to-night and hoped she could continue to come every night and hear Susy pray, as before. Noticing that the child wished to respond but was evidently troubled as to how to word her answer, she asked what the difficulty was. Susy explained that Miss Foote (the governess) had been teaching her about the Indians and their religious beliefs, whereby it appeared that they had not only a god, but several. This had set Susy to thinking. As a result of this thinking she had stopped praying. She qualified this statement—that is, she modified it—saying she did not now pray "in the same way" as she had formerly done. Her mother said, "Tell me about it, dear."

"Well, mamma, the Indians believed they knew, but now we know they were wrong. By and by it can turn out that we are wrong. So now I only pray that there may be a God and a heaven—or something better."

I wrote down this pathetic prayer in its precise wording at the time in a record which we kept of the children's sayings and my reverence for it has grown with the years that have passed over my head since then. Its untaught grace and simplicity are a child's but the wisdom and the pathos of it are of all the ages that have come and gone since the race of man has lived and longed and hoped and feared and doubted.

To go back a year—Susy aged seven. Several times her mother said to her, "There, there, Susy, you mustn't cry over little things."

This furnished Susy a text for thought. She had been breaking her heart over what had seemed vast disasters—a broken toy; a picnic canceled by thunder and lightning and rain; the mouse that was growing tame and friendly in the nursery caught and killed by the cat —and now came this strange revelation. For some unaccountable reason these were not vast calamities. Why? How is the size of calamities measured? What is the rule? There must be some way to tell the great ones from the small ones; what is the law of these proportions? She examined the problem earnestly and long. She gave it her best thought from time to time for two or three days—but it baffled her—defeated her. And at last she gave up and went to her mother for help.

"Mamma, what is 'little things'?"

It seemed a simple question—at first. And yet be-

Susy's chair when she was a child, restored

fore the answer could be put into words, unsuspected and unforseen difficulties began to appear. They increased; they multiplied; they brought about another defeat. The effort to explain came to a standstill. Then Susy tried to help her mother out—with an instance, an example, an illustration. The mother was getting ready to go downtown, and one of her errands was to buy a long-promised toy watch for Susy.

"If you forgot the watch, mamma, would that be a little thing?"

She was not concerned about the watch, for she knew it would not be forgotten. What she was hoping for was that the answer would unriddle the riddle and bring rest and peace to her perplexed little mind.

The hope was disappointed, of course—for the reason that the size of a misfortune is not determinable by an outsider's measurement of it but only by the measurements applied to it by the person specially affected by it. The king's lost crown is a vast matter to the king but of no consequence to the child. The lost toy is a great matter to the child but in the king's eyes it is not a thing to break the heart about. A verdict was reached but it was based upon the above model and Susy was granted leave to measure her disasters thereafter with her own tape-line.

I will throw in a note or two here touching the time when Susy was seventeen. She had written a play modeled upon Greek lines, and she and Clara and Margaret Warner and other young comrades had played it to a charmed houseful of friends in our house in Hartford. Charles Dudley Warner and his brother, George, were present. They were near neighbors and warm friends of ours. They were full of praises of the workmanship of the play, and George Warner came over the next morning and had a long talk with Susy. The result of it was this verdict:

"She is the most interesting person I have ever known, of either sex."

Remark of a lady—Mrs. Cheney, I think, author of the biography of her father, Rev. Dr. Bushnell:

"I made this note after one of my talks with Susy: 'She knows all there is of life and its meanings. She could not know it better if she had lived it out to its limit. Her intuitions and ponderings and analyzings seem to have taught her all that my sixty years have taught me.' "

Remark of another lady; she is speaking of Susy's last days:

"In those last days she walked as if on air, and her walk answered to the buoyancy of her spirits and the passion of intellectual energy and activity that possessed her."

I return now to the point where I made this diversion. From her earliest days, as I have already indicated, Susy was given to examining things and thinking them out by herself. She was not trained to this; it was the make of her mind. In matters involving questions of fair or unfair dealing she reviewed the details patiently and surely arrived at a right and logical conclusion. In Munich, when she was six years old, she was harassed by a recurrent dream, in which a ferocious bear figured. She came out of the dream each time sorely frightened and crying. She set herself the task of analyzing this dream. The reasons of it? The purpose of it? The origin of it? No—the moral aspect of it. Her verdict, arrived at after candid and searching investigation, exposed it to the charge of being one-sided and unfair in its construction: for (as she worded it) *she* was "never the one that ate, but always the one that was eaten."

Susy backed her good judgment in matters of morals with conduct to match—even upon occasions when it caused her sacrifice to do it. When she was six and her sister Clara four, the pair were troublesomely quarrelsome. Punishments were tried as a means of breaking up this custom—these failed. Then rewards were tried. A day without a quarrel brought candy. The children were their own witnesses—each for or against her own self. Once Susy took the candy, hesitated, then returned it with a suggestion that she was not fairly entitled to it. Clara kept hers, so here was a conflict of evidence—one witness *for* a quarrel and one against it. But the better witness of the two was on the affirmative side and the quarrel stood proved and no candy due to either side. There seemed to be no defense for Clara— yet there was and Susy furnished it; and Clara went free. Susy said, "I don't know whether she felt wrong in *her* heart but I didn't feel right in *my* heart."

It was a fair and honorable view of the case and a specially acute analysis of it for a child of six to make. There was no way to convict Clara now, except to put her on the stand again and review her evidence. There was a doubt as to the fairness of this procedure, since her former evidence had been accepted and not challenged at the time. The doubt was examined and canvassed—then she was given the benefit of it and acquitted; which was just as well, for in the meantime she had eaten the candy anyway.

Whenever I think of Susy I think of Marjorie Fleming. There was but one Marjorie Fleming. There can never be another. No doubt I think of Marjorie when I think of Susy mainly because Dr. John Brown, that noble and beautiful soul—rescuer of marvelous Marjorie from oblivion—was Susy's great friend in her babyhood —her worshiper and willing slave.

In 1873, when Susy was fourteen months old, we arrived in Edinburgh from London, fleeing thither for rest and refuge after experiencing what had been to us an entirely new kind of life—six weeks of daily lunches, teas and dinners away from home. We carried no letters of introduction; we hid ourselves away in Veitch's family hotel in George Street and prepared to have a comfortable season all to ourselves. But by good fortune this did not happen. Straightway Mrs. Clemens needed a physician and I stepped around to 23 Rutland Street to see if the author of *Rab and His Friends* was still a practicing physician. He was. He came, and for six weeks thereafter we were together every day, either in his house or in our hotel.

His was a sweet and winning face—as beautiful a face as I have ever known. Reposeful, gentle, benignant —the face of a saint at peace with all the world and placidly beaming upon it the sunshine of love that filled his heart. Doctor John was beloved by everybody in Scotland; and I think that on its downward sweep southward it found no frontier. I think so because when, a few years later, infirmities compelled Doctor John to give up his practice, and Mr. Douglas, the publisher, and other friends set themselves the task of raising a fund of a few thousand dollars, whose income was to be devoted to the support of himself and his maiden sister (who was in age), the fund was not only promptly made up but so *very* promptly that the books were closed before friends a hundred miles south of the line had had an opportunity to contribute. No public appeal was made. The matter was never mentioned in print. Mr. Douglas and the other friends applied for contributions by private letter only. Many complaints came from London and everywhere between from people who had not been allowed an opportunity to contribute. This sort of complaint is so new to the world—so strikingly unusual—that I think it worth while to mention it.

Doctor John was very fond of animals, and particularly of dogs. No one needs to be told this who has read that pathetic and beautiful masterpiece, *Rab and His Friends*. After his death his son, Jock, published a brief memorial of him which he distributed privately among the friends; and in it occurs a little episode which illustrates the relationship that existed between Doctor John and the other animals. It is furnished by an Edinburgh lady whom Doctor John used to pick up and carry to school or back in his carriage frequently at a time when she was twelve years old. She said that they were chatting together tranquilly one day, when he suddenly broke off in the midst of a sentence and thrust his head out of the carriage window eagerly—then resumed his place with a disappointed look on his face. The girl said: "Who is it? Some one you know?" He said, "No, a dog I don't know."

He had two names for Susy—"Wee wifie" and "Megalopis." This formidable Greek title was conferred in honor of her big, big dark eyes. Susy and the Doctor had a good deal of romping together. Daily he unbent his dignity and played "bear" with the child. I do not now remember which of them was the bear but I think it was the child. There was a sofa across a corner of the parlor with a door behind it opening into Susy's quarters and she used to lie in wait for the Doctor behind the sofa—not lie in wait but stand in wait; for you could only get just a glimpse of the top of her yellow head when she stood upright. According to the rules of the game she was invisible and this glimpse did not count. I think she must have been the bear, for I can remember two or three occasions when she sprang out from behind the sofa and surprised the Doctor into frenzies of fright, which were not in the least modified by the fact that he knew that the "bear" was there and was coming.

It seems incredible that Doctor John should ever have wanted to tell a grotesque and rollicking anecdote. Such a thing seems so out of character with that gentle and tranquil nature that—but no matter. I tried to teach him the anecdote and he tried his best for two or three days to perfect himself in it—and he never succeeded. It was the most impressive exhibition that ever was. There was no human being nor dog of his acquaintance in all Edinburgh that would not have been paralyzed with astonishment to step in there and see Doctor John trying to do that anecdote. It was one which I have told some hundreds of times on the platform and which I was always very fond of because it worked the audience so hard. It was a stammering man's account of how he got cured of his infirmity—which was accomplished by introducing a whistle into the midst of every word which he found himself unable to finish on account of the obstruction of the stammering. And so his whole account was an absurd mixture of stammering and whistling—which was irresistible to an audience properly keyed up for laughter. Doctor John learned to do the mechanical details of the anecdote but he was never able to inform these details with expression. He was preternaturally grave and earnest all through, and so when he fetched up with the climaxing triumphant sentence at the end—but I must quote that sentence, or the reader will not understand. It was this:

"The doctor told me that whenever I wanted to sta- (whistle) sta- (whistle) sta- (whistle) *ammer*, I must whistle; and I did, and it k- (whistle) k- (whistle) k- (whistle) k- ured me *entirely!*"

The Doctor could not master that triumphant note. He always gravely stammered and whistled and whistled and stammered it through, and it came out at the end with the solemnity and the gravity of the judge delivering sentence to a man with the black cap on.

He was the loveliest creature in the world—except his aged sister, who was just like him. We made the round of his professional visits with him in his carriage every day for six weeks. He always brought a basket of grapes and we brought books. The scheme which we began with on the first round of visits was the one which was maintained until the end—and was based upon this remark, which he made when he was disembarking from the carriage at his first stopping place to visit a patient, "Entertain yourselves while I go in here and reduce the population."

As a child Susy had a passionate temper; and it cost her much remorse and many tears before she learned to govern it, but after that it was a wholesome salt and her character was the stronger and healthier for its presence. It enabled her to be good with dignity; it preserved her not only from being good for vanity's sake but from even the appearance of it. In looking back over the long-vanished years it seems but natural and excusable that I should dwell with longing affection and preference upon incidents of her young life which made it beautiful to us and that I should let its few and small offenses go unsummoned and unreproached.

In the summer of 1880, when Susy was just eight years of age, the family were at Quarry Farm, on top of a high hill, three miles from Elmira, New York, where we always spent our summers in those days. Hay-cutting time was approaching and Susy and Clara were counting the hours, for the time was big with a great event for them; they had been promised that they might mount the wagon and ride home from the fields on the summit of the hay mountain. This perilous privilege, so dear to their age and species, had never been granted them before. Their excitement had no bounds. They could talk of nothing but this epoch-making adventure now. But misfortune overtook Susy on the very morning of the important day. In a sudden outbreak of passion she corrected Clara—with a shovel or stick or something of the sort. At any rate, the offense committed was of a gravity clearly beyond the limit allowed in the nursery. In accordance with the rule and custom of the house, Susy went to her mother to confess and to help decide upon the size and character of the punishment due. It was quite understood that as a punishment could have but one rational object and function—to act as a reminder and warn the transgressor against transgressing in the same way again—the children would know about as well as any how to choose a penalty which would be rememberable and effective. Susy and her mother discussed various punishments but none of them seemed adequate. This fault was an unusually serious one and required the setting up of a danger signal in the memory that would not blow out nor burn out but remain a fixture there and furnish its saving warning indefinitely. Among the punishments mentioned was deprivation of the hay-wagon ride. It was noticeable that this one hit Susy hard. Finally, in the summing up, the mother named over the list and asked, "Which one do you think it ought to be, Susy?"

Susy studied, shrank from her duty, and asked, "Which do you think, mamma?"

"Well, Susy, I would rather leave it to you. *You* make the choice yourself."

It cost Susy a struggle and much and deep thinking and weighing—but she came out where anyone who knew her could have foretold she would:

"Well, mamma, I'll make it the hay wagon, because, you know, the other things might not make me remember not to do it again, but if I don't get to ride on the hay wagon I can remember it easily."

In this world the real penalty, the sharp one, the lasting one, never falls otherwise than on the wrong person. It was not *I* that corrected Clara but the remembrance of poor Susy's lost hay ride still brings *me* a pang —after twenty-six years.

Apparently Susy was born with humane feelings for the animals and compassion for their troubles. This enabled her to see a new point in an old story, once, when she was only six years old—a point which had been overlooked by older and perhaps duller people for many ages. Her mother told her the moving story of the sale of Joseph by his brethren, the staining of his coat with the blood of the slaughtered kid, and the rest of it. She dwelt upon the inhumanity of the brothers, their cruelty toward their helpless young brother, and the unbrotherly treachery which they practiced upon him; for she hoped to teach the child a lesson in gentle pity and mercifulness which she would remember. Apparently her desire was accomplished, for the tears came into Susy's eyes and she was deeply moved. Then she said, "Poor little kid!"

A child's frank envy of the privileges and distinctions of its elders is often a delicately flattering attention and the reverse of unwelcome, but sometimes the envy is not placed where the beneficiary is expecting it to be placed. Once when Susy was seven she sat breathlessly absorbed in watching a guest of ours adorn herself for a ball. The lady was charmed by this homage, this mute and gentle admiration, and was happy in it. And when her pretty labors were finished and she stood at last perfect, unimprovable, clothed like Solomon in his glory, she paused, confident and expectant, to receive from Susy's tongue the tribute that was burning in her eyes. Susy drew an envious little sigh and said, "I wish *I* could have crooked teeth and spectacles!"

Once, when Susy was six months along in her eighth year, she did something one day in the presence of company which subjected her to criticism and reproof. Afterward, when she was alone with her mother, as was her custom she reflected a little while over the matter. Then she set up what I think—and what the shade of Burns would think—was a quite good philosophical defense: "Well, mamma, you know I didn't see myself and so I couldn't know how it looked."

In homes where the near friends and visitors are mainly literary people—lawyers, judges, professors and clergymen—the children's ears become early familiarized with wide vocabularies. It is natural for them to pick up any words that fall in their way; it is natural for them to pick up big and little ones indiscriminately; it is natural for them to use without fear any word that comes to their net, no matter how formidable it may be as to size. As a result, their talk is a curious and funny musketry-clatter of little words, interrupted at intervals by the heavy-artillery crash of a word of such imposing sound and size that it seems to shake the ground and rattle the windows. Sometimes the child gets a wrong idea of a word which it has picked up by chance, and attaches to it a meaning which impairs its usefulness— but this does not happen as often as one might expect it would. Indeed, it happens with an infrequency which may be regarded as remarkable. As a child, Susy had good fortune with her large words and she employed many of them. She made no more than her fair share of mistakes. Once when she thought something very funny was going to happen (but it didn't) she was racked and torn with laughter, by anticipation. But apparently she still felt sure of her position, for she said, "If it had happened I should have been transformed [transported] with glee."

And earlier, when she was a little maid of five years, she informed a visitor that she had been in a church only once, and that was the time when Clara was "crucified" (christened).

In Heidelberg, when Susy was six, she noticed that the Schloss gardens were populous with snails creeping all about everywhere. One day she found a new dish on her table and inquired concerning it and learned that it was made of snails. She was awed and impressed and said, "Wild ones, mamma?"

She was thoughtful and considerate of others—an acquired quality, no doubt. No one seems to be born with it. One hot day, at home in Hartford, when she was a little child, her mother borrowed her fan several times (a Japanese one, value five cents), refreshed herself with it a moment or two, then handed it back with a word of thanks. Susy knew her mother would use the

Susy in Munich, 1878

fan all the time if she could do it without putting a deprivation upon its owner. She also knew that her mother could not be persuaded to do that. A relief must be devised somehow; Susy devised it. She got five cents out of her money box and carried it to Patrick and asked him to take it downtown (a mile and a half) and buy a Japanese fan and bring it home. He did it—and thus thoughtfully and delicately was the exigency met and the mother's comfort secured. It is to the child's credit that she did not save herself expense by bringing down another and more costly kind of fan from upstairs but was content to act upon the impression that her mother desired the Japanese kind—content to accomplish the desire and stop with that, without troubling about the wisdom or unwisdom of it.

Sometimes while she was still a child her speech fell into quaint and strikingly expressive forms. Once— aged nine or ten—she came to her mother's room when her sister Jean was a baby and said Jean was crying in the nursery and asked if she might ring for the nurse. Her mother asked, "Is she crying hard?"—meaning cross, ugly.

"Well, no, mamma. It is a weary, lonesome cry."

It is a pleasure to me to recall various incidents which reveal the delicacies of feeling which were so considerable a part of her budding character. Such a revelation came once in a way which, while creditable to her heart, was defective in another direction. She was in her eleventh year then. Her mother had been making the Christmas purchases and she allowed Susy to see the presents which were for Patrick's children. Among these was a handsome sled for Jimmy, on which a stag was painted; also in gilt capitals the word "DEER." Susy was excited and joyous over everything until she came to this sled. Then she became sober and silent—yet the sled was the choicest of all the gifts. Her mother was surprised and also disappointed, and said:

"Why, Susy, doesn't it please you? Isn't it fine?"

Susy hesitated and it was plain that she did not want to say the thing that was in her mind. However, being urged, she brought it haltingly out:

"Well, mamma, it *is* fine and of course it *did* cost a good deal—but—but—why should that be mentioned?"

Seeing that she was not understood, she reluctantly pointed to that word "DEER." It was her orthography that was at fault, not her heart. She had inherited both from her mother.

When Susy was thirteen and was a slender little maid with plaited tails of copper-tinged brown hair down her back and was perhaps the busiest bee in the household hive, by reason of the manifold studies, health exercises and recreations she had to attend to, she secretly and of her own motion and out of love added another task to her labors—the writing of a biography of me. She did this work in her bedroom at night and kept her record hidden. After a little the mother discovered it and filched it and let me see it; then told Susy what she had done and how pleased I was and how proud. I remember that time with a deep pleasure. I had had compliments before but none that touched me like this; none that could approach it for value in my eyes. It has kept that place always since. I have had no compliment, no praise, no tribute from any source that was so precious to me as this one was and still is. As I read it *now*, after all these many years, it is still a king's message to me and brings me the same dear surprise it brought me then—with the pathos added of the thought that the eager and hasty hand that sketched it and scrawled it will not touch mine again—and I feel as the humble and unexpectant must feel when their eyes fall upon the edict that raises them to the ranks of the noble.

It is quite evident that several times, at breakfast and dinner, in those long-past days, I was posing for the biography. In fact, I clearly remember that I *was* doing that—and I also remember that Susy detected it. I remember saying a very smart thing, with a good deal of an air, at the breakfast table one morning and that Susy observed to her mother privately a little later that papa was doing that for the biography.

I cannot bring myself to change any line or word in Susy's sketch of me but will introduce passages from it now and then just as they came in—their quaint simplicity out of her honest heart, which was the beautiful heart of a child. What comes from that source has a charm and grace of its own which may transgress all the recognized laws of literature, if it choose, and yet be literature still and worthy of hospitality.

The spelling is frequently desperate but it was Susy's and it shall stand. I love it and cannot profane it. To me it is gold. To correct it would alloy it, not refine it. It would spoil it. It would take from it its freedom and flexibility and make it stiff and formal. Even when it is most extravagant I am not shocked. It is Susy's spelling and she was doing the best she could—and nothing could better it for me.

She learned languages easily; she learned history easily; she learned music easily; she learned all things easily, quickly and thoroughly except spelling. She even learned that after a while. But it would have grieved me but little if she had failed in it—for although good spelling was my one accomplishment I was never able to greatly respect it. When I was a schoolboy sixty years ago* we had two prizes in our school. One was for good spelling, the other for amiability. These things were thin, smooth, silver disks, about the size of a dollar. Upon the one was engraved in flowing Italian script the words "Good Spelling," on the other was engraved the word "Amiability." The holders of these prizes hung them about the neck with a string—and those holders were the envy of the whole school. There wasn't a pupil that wouldn't have given a leg for the privilege of wearing one of them a week, but no pupil ever got a chance except John RoBards and me. John RoBards was eternally and indestructibly amiable. I may even say devilishly amiable; fiendishly amiable; exasperatingly amiable. That was the sort of feeling that we had about that quality of his. So he always wore the amiability medal. I always wore the other medal. That word "always" is a trifle too strong. We lost the medals several times. It was because they became so monotonous. We needed a change—therefore several times we traded medals. It was a satisfaction to John RoBards to *seem* to be a good speller—which he wasn't. And it was a satisfaction to me to seem to be amiable, for a change. But of course these changes could not long endure—for some schoolmate or other would presently notice what had been happening and that schoolmate would not have been human if he had lost any time in reporting this treason. The teacher took the medals away from us at once, of course—and we always had them back again before Fri-

* Written in 1906.

day night. If we lost the medals Monday morning, John's amiability was at the top of the list Friday afternoon when the teacher came to square up the week's account. The Friday-afternoon session always closed with "spelling down." Being in disgrace, I necessarily started at the foot of my division of spellers, but I always slaughtered both divisions and stood alone with the medal around my neck when the campaign was finished. I *did* miss on a word once, just at the end of one of these conflicts, and so lost the medal. I left the first *r* out of February—but that was to accommodate a sweetheart. My passion was so strong just at that time that I would have left out the whole alphabet if the word had contained it.

As I have said before, I never had any large respect for good spelling. That is my feeling yet. Before the spelling-book came with its arbitrary forms, men unconsciously revealed shades of their characters and also added enlightening shades of expression to what they wrote by their spelling, and so it is possible that the spelling-book has been a doubtful benevolence to us.

Susy began the biography in 1885, when I was in the fiftieth year of my age, and she in the fourteenth of hers. She begins in this way:

We are a very happy family! we consist of papa, mamma, Jean Clara and me. It is papa I am writing about, and I shall have no trouble in not knowing what to say about him, as he is a very striking character. Papa's appearance has been discribed many times, but very incorectly; he has beautiful curly grey hair, not any too thick, or any too long, just right; A roman nose, which greatly improves the beauty of his features, kind blue eyes, and a small mustache, he has a wonderfully shaped head, and profile, he has a very good figure in short he is an extrodinarily fine looking man. All his features are perfect exept that he hasn't extrodinary teeth. His complexion is very fair, and he doesn't ware a beard.

He is a very good man, and a very funny one; he *has* got a temper but we all of us have in this family. He is the loveliest man I ever saw, or ever hope to see, and oh *so* absent minded! He does tell perfectly delightful stories, Clara and I used to sit on each arm of his chair, and listen while he told us stories about the pictures on the wall.

I remember the story-telling days vividly. They were a difficult and exacting audience—those little creatures.

Along one side of the library, in the Hartford home, the bookshelves joined the mantelpiece—in fact, there were shelves on both sides of the mantelpiece. On these shelves and on the mantelpiece stood various ornaments. At one end of the procession was a framed oil-painting of a cat's head; at the other end was a head of a beautiful young girl, life size—called Emmeline, be-

We are a very happy family! we consist of papa, mamma, Jean Clara & me. It is papa I am writing about, and I shall have no trouble in not knowing what to say about him, as he is a very striking character. Papa's appearance has been discribed many times but very incorrectly; he has beautiful curly grey hair, not any too thick, or any too long, just right. A roman nose, which greatly improves the beauty of his features, kind blue eyes, and a small muse-tache, he has a wonderfully shaped head, and profile, he has a very good figure in short he is an extrodinarily fine looking man. all his features are perfect exept that he hasn't extrodinary teeth. His complexion is very fair, and he doesn't ware a beard.

He is a very good man, and a very funny one; he has got a temper but we all of us have in this family.

The opening page of Susy's biography (holograph)

Mark Twain at about fifty

cause she looked just about like that—an impressionist water-color. Between the one picture and the other there were twelve or fifteen of the bric-à-brac things already mentioned, also an oil-painting by Elihu Vedder, "The Young Medusa." Every now and then the children required me to construct a romance—always impromptu—not a moment's preparation permitted—

Library mantel, Hartford house

and into that romance I had to get all that bric-à-brac and the three pictures. I had to start always with the cat and finish with Emmeline. I was never allowed the refreshment of a change, end for end. It was not permissi-

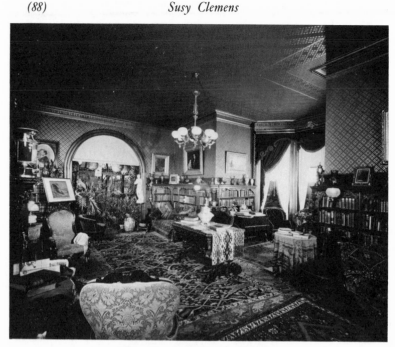

The library, Hartford house

ble to introduce a bric-à-brac ornament into the story
out of its place in the procession.

These bric-à-bracs were never allowed a peaceful
day, a reposeful day, a restful Sabbath. In their lives
there was no Sabbath; in their lives there was no peace;
they knew no existence but a monotonous career of vio-
lence and bloodshed. In the course of time the bric-à-
brac and the pictures showed wear. It was because they
had had so many and such tumultuous adventures in
their romantic careers.

As romancer to the children I had a hard time, even
from the beginning. If they brought me a picture in a
magazine and required me to build a story to it, they
would cover the rest of the page with their pudgy hands

to keep me from stealing an idea from it. The stories
had to be absolutely original and fresh. Sometimes the
children furnished me simply a character or two, or a
dozen, and required me to start out at once on that slim
basis and deliver those characters up to a vigorous and
entertaining life of crime. If they heard of a new trade
or an unfamiliar animal or anything like that, I was
pretty sure to have to deal with those things in the next
romance. Once Clara required me to build a sudden tale
out of a plumber and a "bawgun strictor," and I had to
do it. She didn't know what a boa-constrictor was until
he developed in the tale—then she was better satisfied
with it than ever.

His favorite game is billiards, and when
he is tired, and wishes to rest himself he
stays up all night and plays billiards, it
seems to rest his head. He smokes a great
deal almost incessantly. He has the mind of
an author exactly, some of the simplest
things he can't understand. Our burglar
alarm is often out of order, and papa had
been obliged to take the mahogany room off
from the alarm altogether for a time, because the burglar alarm had been in the
habit of ringing even when the mahogany
room window was closed. At length he
thought that perhaps the burglar alarm
might be in order, and he decided to try and
see; accordingly he put it on, and then went

The billiard room, Hartford house

down and opened the window, consequently the alarm bell rang, it would even if
the alarm had been in order. Papa went de-
spairingly up stairs, and said to mamma,
"Livy the mahogany room wont go on, I
have just opened the window to see." "Why
Youth" mamma replied, "if you've opened
the window why of coarse the alarm will
ring." "That's what I've opened it for, why

I just went down to see if it would ring!"
Mamma tried to explain to papa that when
he wanted to go and see whether the alarm
would ring while the window was closed,
he mustn't go and open the window. But in
vain, papa couldn't understand, and got
very impatient with mamma for trying to
make him believe an impossible thing true.

This is a frank biographer and an honest one; she
uses no sandpaper on me. I have to this day the same
dull head in the matter of conundrums and perplexities
which Susy had discovered in those long-gone days.
Complexities annoy me; they irritate me; then this pro-
gressive feeling presently warms into anger. I cannot
get far in the reading of the commonest and simplest
contract—with its "parties of the first part" and "parties of the second part" and "parties of the third part"—
before my temper is all gone. Ashcroft* comes up here
every day and pathetically tries to make me understand
the points of the lawsuit which we are conducting
against Henry Butters, Harold Wheeler and the rest of
those Plasmon buccaneers, but daily he has to give it up.
It is pitiful to see, when he bends his earnest and ap-
pealing eyes upon me and says after one of his efforts,
"Now you *do* understand *that*, don't you?"

I am always obliged to say, "I *don't*, Ashcroft. I
wish I could understand it but I don't. Send for the
cat."

In the days which Susy is talking about, a perplex-

* One of Mark Twain's secretaries.

ity fell to my lot one day. F. G. Whitmore was my business agent and he brought me out from town in his buggy. We drove by the porte-cochère and toward the stable. Now this was a *single* road and was like a spoon whose handle stretched from the gate to a great round flower bed in the neighborhood of the stable. At the approach to the flower bed the road divided and circumnavigated it, making a loop, which I have likened to the bowl of the spoon. I was sitting on the starboard side. As we neared the loop, I sitting as I say on the starboard side (and that was the side on which the house was), I saw that Whitmore was laying his course to port and was going to start around that spoon bowl on that left-hand side. I said: "Don't do that, Whitmore; take the right-hand side. Then I shall be next to the house when we get to the door."

He said: "*That* will happen in *any* case. It doesn't make any difference which way I go around this flower bed."

I explained to him that he was an ass but he stuck to his proposition, and I said, "Go on and try it and see."

He went on and tried it and sure enough he fetched me up at the door on the very side that he had said I would be. I was not able to believe it then and I don't believe it yet.

I said: "Whitmore, that is merely an accident. You can't do it again." He said he could—and he drove down into the street, fetched around, came back, and actually did it again. I was stupefied, paralyzed, petrified with these strange results but they did not convince me. I didn't believe he could do it another time but he did. He said he could do it all day and fetch up the same way every time. By that time my temper was gone and I asked him to go home and apply to the asylum and I would pay the expenses. I didn't want to see him any more for a week.

I went upstairs in a rage and started to tell Livy about it, expecting to get her sympathy for me and to breed aversion in her for Whitmore; but she merely burst into peal after peal of laughter as the tale of my adventure went on, for her head was like Susy's. Riddles and complexities had no terrors for it. Her mind and Susy's were analytical. I have tried to make it appear that mine was different. Many and many a time I have told that buggy experiment, hoping against hope that I would some time or other find somebody who would be on my side—but it has never happened. And I am never able to go glibly forward and state the circumstances of that buggy's progress without having to halt and consider and call up in my mind the spoon handle, the bowl of the spoon, the buggy and the horse, and my position in the buggy—and the minute I have got that far and try to turn it to the left, it goes to ruin. I can't see how it is ever going to fetch me out right when we get to the door. Susy is right in her estimate. I can't understand things.

That burglar alarm which Susy mentions led a gay and careless life and had no principles. It was generally out of order at one point or another and there was plenty of opportunity, because all the windows and doors in the house, from the cellar up to the top floor, were connected with it. However, in its seasons of being out of order it could trouble us for only a very little while: we quickly found out that it was fooling us and that it was buzzing its blood-curdling alarm merely for

The Clemenses on the *ombra* of their Hartford house

its own amusement. Then we would shut it off and send
to New York for the electrician—there not being one in
all Hartford in those days. When the repairs were finished we would set the alarm again and reestablish our
confidence in it. It never did any real business except
upon one single occasion. All the rest of its expensive
career was frivolous and without purpose. Just that one
time it performed its duty, and its whole duty—gravely,
seriously, admirably. It let fly about two o'clock one
black and dreary March morning and I turned out
promptly, because I knew that it was not fooling this
time. The bathroom door was on my side of the bed. I
stepped in there, turned up the gas, looked at the an-
nunciator, turned off the alarm—so far as the door indicated was concerned—thus stopping the racket. Then I
came back to bed. Mrs. Clemens opened the debate:

"What was it?"

"It was the cellar door."

"Was it a burglar, do you think?"

"Yes," I said, "of course it was. Did you suppose it
was a Sunday-school superintendent?"

"No. What do you suppose he wants?"

"I suppose he wants jewelry, but he is not acquainted with the house and he thinks it is in the cellar.
I don't like to disappoint a burglar whom I am not acquainted with and who has done me no harm, but if he
had had common sagacity enough to inquire, I could
have told him we kept nothing down there but coal and
vegetables. Still, it may be that he *is* acquainted with
this place and that what he really wants is coal and vegetables. On the whole, I think it is vegetables he is after."

"Are you going down to see?"

The Hartford house, probably in the 1880s

"No. I could not be of any assistance. Let him select for himself; I don't know where the things are."

Then she said, "But suppose he comes up to the ground floor!"

"That's all right. We shall know it the minute he opens a door on that floor. It will set off the alarm."

Just then the terrific buzzing broke out again. I said: "He has arrived. I told you he would. I know all about burglars and their ways. They are systematic people."

I went into the bathroom to see if I was right, and I was. I shut off the dining-room and stopped the buzzing and came back to bed. My wife said:

"What do you suppose he is after now?"

I said, "I think he has got all the vegetables he wants and is coming up for napkin rings and odds and ends for the wife and children. They all have families—burglars have—and they are always thoughtful of them, always take a few necessaries of life for themselves, and fill out with tokens of remembrance for the family. In taking them they do not forget us: those very things represent tokens of his remembrance of us, and also of our remembrance of him. We never get them again; the memory of the attention remains embalmed in our hearts."

"Are you going down to see what it is he wants now?"

A modern view of the Hartford house

"No," I said; "I am no more interested than I was before. They are experienced people—burglars; *they* know what they want. I should be no help to him. I *think* he is after ceramics and bric-à-brac and such things. If he knows the house he knows that that is all that he can find on the dining-room floor."

She said, with a strong interest perceptible in her tone, "Suppose he comes up here!"

I said, "It is all right. He will give us notice."

"What shall we do then?"

"Climb out of the window."

She said, a little restively, "Well, what is the use of a burglar alarm for us?"

"You have seen, dear heart, that it has been useful up to the present moment, and I have explained to you how it will be continuously useful after he gets up here."

That was the end of it. He didn't ring any more alarms.

Presently I said, "He is disappointed, I think. He has gone off with the vegetables and the bric-à-brac and I think he is dissatisfied."

We went to sleep and at a quarter before eight in the morning I was out and hurrying, for I was to take the 8:29 train for New York. I found the gas burning brightly—full head—all over the first floor. My new overcoat was gone; my old umbrella was gone; my new patent-leather shoes, which I had never worn, were gone. The large window which opened into the ombra at the rear of the house was standing wide. I passed out through it and tracked the burglar down the hill through the trees; tracked him without difficulty, because he had blazed his progress with imitation-silver

napkin rings and my umbrella, and various other things
which he had disapproved of; and I went back in triumph and proved to my wife that he *was* a disappointed
burglar. I had suspected he would be, from the start,
and from his not coming up to our floor to get human
beings.

He has a peculiar gait we like, it seems
just to sute him, but most people do not; he
always walks up and down the room while
thinking and between each coarse at meals.

A lady distantly related to us came to visit us once
in those days. She came to stay a week but all our efforts
to make her happy failed and we could not imagine
why, and she got up her anchor and sailed the next
morning. We did much guessing but could not solve the
mystery. Later we found out what the trouble was. It
was my tramping up and down between the courses.
She conceived the idea that I could not stand her society.

That word "Youth," as the reader has perhaps already guessed, was my wife's pet name for me. It was
gently satirical but also affectionate. I had certain
mental and material peculiarities and customs proper to
a much younger person than I was.

He is very fond of animals particularly cats,
we had a dear little grey kitten once, that he
named "Lazy" (papa always wares grey to
match his hair and eyes) and he would carry

him around on his shoulder, it was a mighty pretty sight! the grey cat sound asleep against papa's grey coat and hair. The names that he has given our different cats, are realy remarkably funny, they are namely "Stray Kit," "Abner" "Motly," "Freulein," Lazy" "Bufalo Bill" and "Soapy Sal" "Cleveland," "Sour Mash" and "Famine"

At one time when the children were small we had a very black mother-cat named Satan, and Satan had a small black offspring named Sin. Pronouns were a difficulty for the children. Little Clara came in one day, her black eyes snapping with indignation, and said: "Papa, Satan ought to be punished. She is out there at the greenhouse and there she stays and stays, and his kitten is downstairs, crying."

Papa uses very strong language, but I have an idea not nearly so strong as when he first married mamma. A lady aquaintance of his is rather apt to interupt what one is saying, and papa told mamma that he thought he should say to the lady's husband "I am glad Mrs. _____ wasn't present when the Deity said ' "let ther be light" ' "

It is as I have said before. This is a frank historian.
She doesn't cover up one's deficiences but gives them an
equal showing with one's handsomer qualities. Of
course I made the remark which she has quoted—and
even at this distant day I am still as much as half persuaded that if that lady mentioned had been present
when the Creator said "Let there be light" she would
have interrupted him and we shouldn't ever have got it.

Papa said the other day, "I am a mugwump and a mugwump is pure from the
marrow out." (Papa knows that I am writing this biography of him, and he said this
for it.) He doesn't like to go to church at all,
why I never understood, until just now, he
told me the other day, that he couldn't bear
to hear any one talk but himself, but that he
could listen to himself talk for hours without getting tired, of course he said this in
joke, but I've no dought it was founded on
truth."

Susy's remark about my strong language troubles
me and I must go back to it. All through the first ten
years of my married life I kept a constant and discreet
watch upon my tongue while in the house, and went
outside and to a distance when circumstances were too
much for me and I was obliged to seek relief. I prized
my wife's respect and approval above all the rest of the
human race's respect and approval. I dreaded the day

when she should discover that I was but a whited sepul-
cher partly freighted with suppressed language. I was
so careful, during ten years, that I had not a doubt that
my suppressions had been successful. Therefore I was
quite as happy in my guilt as I could have been if I had
been innocent.

But at last an accident exposed me. I went into the
bathroom one morning to make my toilet and carelessly
left the door two or three inches ajar. It was the first
time that I had ever failed to take the precaution of
closing it tightly. I knew the necessity of being particular about this, because shaving was always a trying
ordeal for me, and I could seldom carry it through to a
finish without verbal helps. Now this time I was unpro-
tected and did not suspect it. I had no extraordinary
trouble with my razor on this occasion and was able to
worry through with mere mutterings and growlings of
an improper sort but with nothing noisy or emphatic
about them—no snapping and barking. Then I put on a
shirt. My shirts are an invention of my own. They open
in the back and are buttoned there—when there are but-
tons. This time the button was missing. My temper
jumped up several degrees in a moment and my remarks rose accordingly, both in loudness and vigor of
expression. But I was not troubled, for the bathroom
door was a solid one and I supposed it was firmly closed.
I flung up the window and threw the shirt out. It fell
upon the shrubbery where the people on their way to
church could admire it if they wanted to; there was
merely fifty feet of grass between the shirt and the
passer-by. Still rumbling and thundering distantly, I
put on another shirt. Again the button was absent. I
augmented my language to meet the emergency and

threw that shirt out of the window. I was too angry—
too insane—to examine the third shirt, but put it furi-
ously on. Again the button was absent, and that shirt
followed its comrades out of the window. Then I
straightened up, gathered my reserves, and let myself
go like a cavalry charge. In the midst of that great as-
sault my eye fell upon that gaping door and I was paralyzed.

   It took me a good while to finish my toilet. I extended the time unnecessarily in trying to make up my
mind as to what I would best do in the circumstances. I
tried to hope that Mrs. Clemens was asleep but I knew
better. I could not escape by the window. It was narrow
and suited only to shirts. At last I made up my mind to
boldly loaf through the bedroom with the air of a person who had not been doing anything. I made half the
journey successfully. I did not turn my eyes in her direction, because that would not be safe. It is very difficult to look as if you have not been doing anything
when the facts are the other way, and my confidence in
my performance oozed steadily out of me as I went
along. I was aiming for the left-hand door because it
was farthest from my wife. It had never been opened
from the day that the house was built but it seemed a
blessed refuge for me now. The bed was this one,
wherein I am lying now and dictating these histories
morning after morning with so much serenity.* It was
this same old elaborately carved black Venetian bedstead—the most comfortable bedstead that ever was,
with space enough in it for a family, and carved angels
enough surmounting its twisted columns and its headboard and footboard to bring peace to the sleepers, and

   * Written in 1906.

pleasant dreams. I had to stop in the middle of the room. I hadn't the strength to go on. I believed that I was under accusing eyes—that even the carved angels were inspecting me with an unfriendly gaze. You know how it is when you are convinced that somebody behind you is looking steadily at you. You *have* to turn your face—you can't help it. I turned mine. The bed was placed as it is now, with the foot where the head ought to be. If it had been placed as it should have been, the high headboard would have sheltered me. But the footboard was no sufficient protection and I could be seen over it. I was exposed. I was wholly without protection. I turned, because I couldn't help it—and my memory of what I saw is still vivid after all these years.

Against the white pillows I saw the black head—I saw that young and beautiful face; and I saw the gracious eyes with a something in them which I had never seen there before. They were snapping and flashing with indignation. I felt myself crumbling; I felt myself shrinking away to nothing under that accusing gaze. I stood silent under that desolating fire for as much as a minute, I should say—it seemed a very, very long time. Then my wife's lips parted and from them issued—*my latest bathroom remark*. The language perfect, but the expression velvety, unpractical, apprentice-like, ignorant, inexperienced, comically inadequate, absurdly weak and unsuited to the great language. In my life time I had never heard anything so out of tune, so inharmonious, so incongruous, so ill suited to each other as were those mighty words set to that feeble music. I tried to keep from laughing, for I was a guilty person in deep need of charity and mercy. I tried to keep from burst-

The Clemenses on the *ombra* of their Hartford house (another view)

ing, and I succeeded—until she gravely said, "There, now you know how it sounds."

Then I exploded; the air was filled with my fragments and you could hear them whiz. I said, "Oh, Livy, if it sounds like that, God forgive me, I will never do it again!"

Then she had to laugh herself. Both of us broke into convulsions and went on laughing until we were physically exhausted and spiritually reconciled.

The children were present at breakfast—Clara, aged six, and Susy, eight—and the mother made a guarded remark about strong language; guarded because she did not wish the children to suspect anything —a guarded remark which censured strong language. Both children broke out in one voice with this comment: "Why, mamma, papa uses it!" I was astonished. I had supposed that that secret was safe in my own breast and that its presence had never been suspected. I asked, "How did you know, you little rascals?"

"Oh," they said, "we often listen over the balusters when you are in the hall explaining things to George."

One of his latest books was the "Prince and the Pauper" and it is unquestionably the best book he has ever written, some people want him to keep to his old style, some gentleman wrote him, "I enjoyed "Huckelberry Finn" immensly and am glad to see that you have returned to your old style". . . . . That enoyed me greatly, because it trobles me* to have so few people know papa, I mean realy know him, they think of Mark Twain as a humorist joking at every thing; "and with a mop of reddish brown hair, which sorely needs the barbar's brush, a roman nose, short stubby mustache, a sad care-worn face, with many

* Susy was troubled by that word, and uncertain; she wrote a *u* above it in the proper place, but reconsidered the matter and struck it out. SLC

crow's feet," etc. that is the way people picture papa, I have wanted papa to write a
book that would reveal something of his
kind sympathetic nature, and the "Prince
and Pauper" partly does it. The book is full
is full of lovely charming ideas, and oh the
language! it is perfect, I think. I think that
one of the most touching scenes in it, is
where the pauper is riding on horsback
with his nobles in the recognition procession, and he sees his mother, oh and then
what followed; how she runs to his side,
when she sees him throw up his hand palm
outward, and is rudely pushed off by one of
the king's officers and then how the little
pauper's consience troubles him as he
rembers the shameful words that were falling from his lips, when she was torn from
his side. "I know you not woman" And how
his grandeurs were stricken valueless, and
his pride consumed to ashes.

It is a wonderfully beautiful and touching little scene, and papa has described it so
wonderfully. I never saw a man with so
much variety and feeling as papa has; now
the "Prince and the Pauper" is full of
touching places, but there is most always a
streak of humor in there somewhere now in

Susy at about the time she was writing the biography

the "Coronation" in the stirring coronation, just after the little king has got his crown back again papa brings that in about the seal, where the Pauper says he used the seal "to crack nuts with," oh it is so funny and nice! papa very seldom writes a passage without Some humorisam in it some where, and I don't think he ever will.

The children always helped their mother to edit

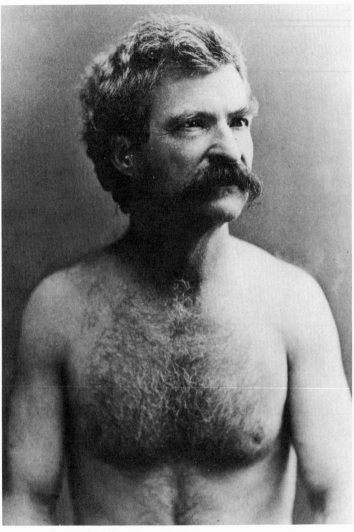

Mark Twain at about fifty

my books in manuscript. She would sit on the porch at
the farm and read aloud, with her pencil in her hand,
and the children would keep an alert and suspicious eye

upon her right along, for the belief was well grounded in them that whenever she came across a particularly satisfactory passage she would strike it out. Their suspicions were well founded. The passages which were so satisfactory to them always had an element of strength in them which sorely needed modification or expurgation, and was always sure to get it at their mother's hand. For my own entertainment and to enjoy the protests of the children, I often abused my editor's innocent confidence. I often interlarded remarks of a studied and felicitously atrocious character purposely to achieve the children's brief delight and then see the remorseless pencil do its fatal work. I often joined my supplications to the children's for mercy and strung the argument out and pretended to be in earnest. They were deceived and so was their mother. It was three against one and most unfair. But it was very delightful and I could not resist the temptation. Now and then we gained the victory and there was much rejoicing. Then I privately struck the passage out myself. It had served its purpose. It had furnished three of us with good entertainment, and in being removed from the book by me it was only suffering the fate originally intended for it.

"Papa was born in Misouri, his mother is Grandma Clemens (Jane Lampton Clemens,) of Kentucky, Grandpa Clemen's was one of the F.F.V's of Virginie. Clara and I are sure that papa played the trick on grandma, about the whipping that is related in "The Adventures of Tom Sayer" "Hand

me that switch." The switch hovered in the
air the peril was desperate—"my, look behind you aunt"! The old lady whirled
round and snatched her skirts out of danger. The lad fled on the instant, scrambled
up the high board fence, and dissapeared
over it."* And we know papa played
"Hookey" all the time and how readily
would papa have pretended to be dying so
as not to have to go to school!

These revelations and exposures are searching but
they are just. If I am as transparent to other people as I
was to Susy I have wasted much effort in this life.

Grandma couldn't make papa go to
school, so she let him go into a printing office to learn the trade. He did so, and gradually picked up enough education to enable
him to do about as well as those who were
more studious in early life.

It is noticeable that Susy does not get overheated
when she is complimenting me but maintains a proper
judicial and biographical calm. It is noticeable also and
it is to her credit as a biographer that she distributes
compliment and criticism with a fair and even hand.

* Susy and Clara were quite right about that. SLC

He was about 20 years old when he went on
the Mississippi as a pilot. Just befor he
started on his tripp Mrs. Clemens asked
him to promise her on the Bible not to
touch intoxicating liquors or swear, and he
said "Yes mother I will", and he kept that
promise seven years, when Grandma released him from it. After papa had been a
pilot on the Mississippi, for a time, Uncle
Orion Clemens, was appointed secretary of
the State of Nevada, and papa went with
him out to Nevada to be his secratary. Afterwards he became interested in mining in
California, then he reported for a newspaper, and was on several newspapers; then he
was sent to the Sandwich Islands to _____.*
After that he came back to America and his
friends wanted him to lecture, so he lec-
tured; then he went to Philidelphia, and
found a situation in a printing office; Then
he went abroad on "the Quaker City," and
on board that ship he became equainted
with Uncle Charlie, Mr. C. J. Langdon of
New York, papa and uncle Charlie soon became friends, and when they returned from
their journey, Grandpa Langdon, unce

* —to write some letters concerning the sugar industry for the
Sacramento *Union.* SLC

Charlie's father, told uncle Charlie to invite
Mr. Clemens to dine with them at the St.
Nicholas hotel N.Y. Papa accepted the invitation, and went to dine at the "St. Nicholas" with Grandpapa, and there he met
mamma, Olivia Louise Langdon, first. But
they did not meet again until the next August; because papa went away to California,
and there wrote the "Inocense Abroad."

Mamma was the daughter of Mr. Jervis
Langdon. (I don't know whether Grandpa
had a middle name or not)* and Mrs. Olivia
Lewis Langdon, of Elmira New York. She
had one brother, and one sister, uncle Charlie, Charles J. Langdon; and aunt Susie, Susan Langdon Crane. Mamma loved Grandpapa more than any one else in all the
world, he was her idol, and she his, I think
mamma's love for Grandpa must have very
much resembled, my love for mamma.
Grandpa was a great and good man, and we
all think of him with respect, and love.†

Mamma was an invalid when she was
young, and haud to give up study a long
time.

* He had none. SLC
   † Susy's word "idol" is not misused. The love felt in all three
instances was an enduring passion rightly describable as worship,
idolatry. SLC

Soon papa [came] back east, and papa and mamma were married. Papa wrote mamma a great many beautiful love letters when he was engaged to mamma, but mamma says I am too young to see them yet; I asked papa what I should do for I didn't [know] how I could write a Biography of him without his love-letters, papa said that I could write mamma's oppinion of them, and that would do just as well. So I will do as papa says and mamma says she thinks they are the loveliest love-letters that ever were written, she says she thinks that Hawthorne's love-letters to Mrs. Hawthorne are far inferior to these. Mamma and papa were going to board first in Bufalo, and Grandpa said he would find them a good boarding house. But he afterwards told mamma that he had bought a pretty house for them, and had it all beautifully furnished, he had also hired a young coachman,* and had bought a horse for them, which all would be ready waiting for them, when they should arive in Bufalo; but he wanted to keep it a secret, from "Youth" as Grandpa called papa. What a delightful sur-

* Patrick McAleer. He remained in our service 22 years. SLC

Patrick McAleer, Mark Twain's coachman

prise it was! Grandpa went down to Bufalo with mamma and papa. And when they drove up to the house, papa said he thought the landlord of such a boarding house must charge a great deal, to those who wanted to live there. And when the secret was told papa was delighted beyond all degree.

Mamma has told me the story many times, and I asked her what papa said, when Grandpa told him that the delightful boarding house was his home, mamma answered that he was rather embariesed and so delighted he didn't know what to say. About 6 months after papa and mamma were married Grandpapa died, it was a terrible blow on mamma, and papa told aunt Sue he thought Livy would never smile again she was so broken hearted. Mamma couldn't have had a greater sorrow than that of dear Grandpapa's death, or any that could equal it exept the death of papa. Mamma helped take care of Grandpapa during his illness, and she couldn't give up hope till the end had realy come.* After that she went back to Bufalo; and a few months after dear little Langdon was born.† Mama named him Langdon after Grandpapa, he was a wonderfully beautiful little boy, but very, very delicate. He had wonderful blue eyes, but such a blue that mamma has never been able to discribe them to me, so that I could see them clearly in my mind's eye. His delicate health was a constant anxiety to

* August 6, 1870. SLC
† Nov. 7, 1870. SLC

mamma, and he was so good and sweet, that
that must have troubled her too, as I know
it did. While a little baby he used to carry a
pencil in his little hand, that was his great
plaything; I believe he was very seldom
seen without one in his hand. When he was
in aunt Susy's arms, and would want to go
to mamma he would hold out his hands to
her with the backs of his hands out toward
her, instead of with his palmes out. About a
year* after Langdon was born, I was born,
and my chief occupation then was to cry so
I must have added greatly to mamma's care!
Soon after little Langdon was born, papa
and mamma moved to Hartford to live.
Their house in Bufalo reminded them too
much of dear Grandpapa, so they moved to
Hartford Soon after he died. Soon after little Langdon was born a friend of mamma's
came to visit her (Emma Nigh.)† And she
was taken with the typhoid fever, while visiting mamma. At length she became so de-
lirious, and was so hard to take care of, that
mamma had to send to some of her friends
in Elmira N.Y. to come and help take care
of her. Aunt Clara, came (Miss Clara L.

* [and 5 months] SLC
† Nye. SLC

Spaulding)* she is no relation of hours but we call her aunt Clara, because she is such a great friend of mamma's. She came and helped mamma take care of Emma Nigh, but inspite of all the good care that she received, she grew worse and died. Just after I mentioned, that mamma and papa couldn't stay in their house in Bufalo because it reminded so much of Grandpapa, mamma received a letter from aunt Susy, in which aunt Susy says a good deal about Grandpapa, and the letter shows so clearly how much every one that knew Grandpapa loved and respected him; that mamma let me take it to copy what is in it about Grandpapa, And mamma thought it would fit in nicely here.

The Farm, April 16th/85
"Livy dear,
Are you not reminded by todays report of Gen. Grant of father? You remember how as Judge Smith and others whom father had chosen as executors were going out of the room, he said "Gentlemen I shall live to bury you all," smiled and was cheerful.

* Now Mrs. John B. Stanchfield. SLC

At that time he had far less strength than
Gen. Grant seems to have, but that same
wonderful courage to battle with the foe.
All along, there has been much to remind
me of father, of his quiet patience—in Gen.
Grant. There certainly is a marked likeness
in the souls of the two men. Watching day
by day the reports from the nations sick
room brings to mind so vividly the days of
the summer of 1870. And yet they seem so
far away, I seemed as a child compared with
now, both in years and experiance. The best
and the hardest of life have been since then,
to me, and I know this is so in your life. All
before seems dreamy—I sepose this [was]
because our lives had to be all readjusted to
go on without that great power in them. Father was quietly such a power in so many
lives beside ours Livy dear,—not in kind or
degree the same to any one, but oh a power!
the evening of the last company, I was so
struck with the fact, when Mr. Atwater
stood quietly before fathers portrait a long
time, and turning to me said, "we shall
never see his like again"—with a tremble
and a choking in his voice,—this after 15
yrs. and from a business friend. And some

stranger a week ago spoke of his habit of giving as so remarkable, he having heard of father's generosity" x x x x x x x x

Papa made arrangements to read at Vassar College the 1st of May, and I went with him. We went by way of N.Y. City; Mamma went with us to New York and stayed two days, to do some shopping. We started Tuesday at 1/2 past two o'clock in the after noon, and reached New York about 1/4 past 6. Papa went right up to Gen. Grants from the station and mamma, and I went to the Everett House. Aunt Clara came to supper with us up in our room. We were going to the theater right after supper, and we expected papa to take us there, and to come home as early as he could. But we got through dinner, and he didn't come, and didn't come, and mamma got more perplexed and worried, but at last we thought we would have to go without him, so we put on our things, and started down stairs but before we'd gotten half down, we met papa coming up, with a great bunch of roses in his hand, he explained that the reason he was so late was that his watch stopped, and

he didn't notice, and kept thinking it an
hour earlier than it realy was. The roses he
carried were some Col. [Fred] Grant sent to
mamma. We went to the theater and enjoyed "Adonis," the pals acted very much,
we reached home about 1/2 past 11 o'clock,
and went right to bed. Wed. morning we
got up rather late, and had breakfast about
1/2 past 9 o'clock. After breakfast mamma
went out shopping, and papa and I went to
see papa's agent about some business matters. After papa had gotten through talking
to cousin Charlie, his agent, we went to get
a friend of papa's (Major Pond,) to go and
see a dog show with us. Then we went to
see the dogs with Major Pond, and we had a
delightful time seing so many dogs together; when we got through seeing the
dogs, papa thought he would go up and see
Gen. Grant, and I went with him,—this
was April 29th 1885. Papa went up into
Gen. Grant's room, and he took me with
him, I felt greatly honored and delighted
when papa took me into Gen. Grant's room
and let me see the Gen. and Col. Grant; for
Gen. Grant is a man I shall be glad all my
life that I have seen. Papa and Gen. Grant

had a long talk together; and papa has writen an account of his talk and visit with Gen. Grant for me to put into this Biography.

<u>1885</u>

"April 29th 1885. "I called on Gen. Grant and took Susie* with me. The Gen. was looking and feeling far better, than he had looked or felt for some months. He had so ventured to work again on his book that morning—the first time he had done any work for perhaps a month. This morning's work was his first attempt at dictating and it was a thourough success to his great delight. He had always said that it would be impossible for him to dictate anything; but I had said that he was noted for clearness of statement, and a narative was simply a statement of consecutive facts and that he was consequently peculiarly qualified and equipped for dictation. This turned out to be true; for he had dictated two hours that morning to a short hand writer, had never hessitated for words, had not repeated him-

* As I have mentioned in my introduction, in her early years Clemens spelled her name in this way. CN

self, and the manuscript, when finished needed no revision. The two hours work was an account of Appomatox, and this was such an extremely important feature, that his book would necessarily have been severely lame without it. Therefore I had taken a short hand writer there before to see if I could not get him to write at least a few lines about Appomatox;* but he was at that time, not well enough to undertake it. I was aware that of all the hundred versions of Appomatox, not one was realy corect. Therefore I was extremely anxious that he should leave behind him the truth. His throat was not disstressing him and his voice was much better and stronger than usual. He was so delighted to have got Appomatox, accomplished, once more in his life—to have got the matter off his mind— that he was as talkative as his old self. He received Susy very pleasantly, and then fell to talking about certain matters which he hoped to be able to dictate next day; and he said in substance, that—among other things —he wanted to settle once for all a question that had been bandied about from mouth to

* I was his publisher. I was putting his "Personal Memoirs" to press at the time. SLC

mouth and from newspaper to newspaper to newspaper, and that question was: with whom orriginated the idea of the March to the Sea,—was it Grant's or was it Sherman's idea?

Whether I or some one else—being anxious to get the important fact settled—asked him with whom the idea orriginated, I dont remember, but I remember his answer, I shall always remember his answer.

Gen. Grant said. "Neither of us orriginated the idea of Shermans march to the sea. The Enemy did it."

He went on to say that the enemy very necessarily orriginates a great many of the plans that the General on the opposite side gets the credit for, at the same time the enemy is doing that, he is laying open other moves, which the General sees and takes advantage of.

In this case Sherman had a plan all thought out of course. He meant to destroy the two remaining railroads in that part of the country and that would have finished up that region. But Gen. How* did not play the military part that he was expected to

* Hood. SLC

play. On the contrary Gen. How made a dive Chattanooga. This left the march to the sea open to Sherman. And so after sending part of his army do defend and hold what he had conquered in the Chattanooga region, he was perfectly free to proceed with the rest of it through Georgia. He saw the opportunity and he would not have beene fit for his place, if he had not seized it.

"He wrote me, (the Gen. is speaking) what his plan was, and I sent him word to go ahead. My staff were opposed to the movement," (I think he said it tried to persuade him to stop Sherman) The of his staff the Gen. said even went so far, as to go to Washington without the General's knowledge, and get the ear of the authaurities, and he succeeded in erasing [arousing] their fears to such an extent that they telegraphed me to stop Sherman.

Out of deferance to the goverment I telegraphed Sherman and stopped him twenty four hours; and then considering that that was deferance enough to the government, I telegraphed him to go ahead again."

I have not tried to give the Generals language but only the general idea of what he said.

The thing that mainly struck me was his terse remark that the enemy orriginated the idea of the march to the sea.

It struck me because it was so suggestive of the generals epigramatic fassion—saying a great deal, in a single crisp sentence."

Mark Twain

After papa and Gen. Grant had, had their talk, we went back to the hotel where mamma was, and papa told mamma all about his interview with Gen. Grant. Mamma and I had a nice quiet afternoon together;* and papa went to read in public; there were a great many authors that read that Thursday afternoon beside papa; I would have liked to have gone and heard papa read, but papa said he was going to read in Vasser just just what he was planning to read in New York. So I staid at home with mamma. The next day mamma planned to take the four o'clock car back to Hartford. We rose quite early that morning and went to the "Viennia Bakery" and took

* They always shut themselves up together when there was an opportunity to have what Susy called "a cosy time." SLC

breakfast there. From there we went to a German book store, and bought some German books for Clara's birth day. Then mamma and I went to do some shopping, and papa went to see Gen. Grant. After we had finished doing our shopping, we went home to the hotel together. When we entered our rooms in the hotel, we saw on the table a vase full of exquisett red roses. Mamma who is very fond of flowers, exclaimed, "Oh I wonder who could have sent them"? We both looked at the card in the midst of the roses, and saw that it was written on in papa's hand writing, it was written in German. "Liebes Geschenk on die Mamma".* Mamma was delighted. Papa came home, and give mamma her ticket; and after visiting a while with her, went to see Maj. Pond, and mamma and I sat down to our lunch. After lunch most of our time was taken up with packing. And at about 3 o'clock, we went to escort mamma to the train. We got on board the train with her, and stayed with her about 5 minutes; and then we said good bye to her and the train started for Hartford. It was the first time I had ever beene away from home without

* "Loving gift to Mamma." CN

mamma in my life, although I was 13 yrs. old. Papa and I rode back to the hotel, and got Maj. Pond, and then went to see the "Brooklyn Bridge" we went across it to Brooklyn on the cars, and then walked back across it from Brooklyn to New York. We enjoyed looking at the beautiful scenery, and we could see the bridge moove under the intense heat of the sun. We had a perfectly delightful time, but wer pretty tired when we got back to the hotel. Maj. Pond, and Miss Jessie, a friend of his took dinner with us up in our hotel rooms. They left a little while, after we had finished dinner and then papa and I went to bed. The next morning we rose early, took our breakfast and took an early train to Poughkeepsie. We had a very pleasant journey to Poughkeepsie, the Hudson, was magnificent shrouded with beautiful mists. When we arived at Poughkeepsie, it was raining quite hard; which fact greatly dissapointed me, because I very much wanted to see the outside of the buildings of Vassar College, and as it rained, that would be impossible.

It was quite a long drive from the station to Vassar College, and papa and I had a nice long time to discuss and laugh over German profanity. One of the German frases papa particularly enjoys is, "Ah heilige Maria, Mutter jesus"!* Jean has a german nurse and this was one of her phrases, there was a time when Jean exclaimed: "Ach Gott!"† to every trifle, but when mamma found it out, she was shocked and instantly put a stop to it.

We at length reached Vassar College, and she looked very finely, her buildings and her grounds being very beautiful. We went to the front doore and rang the bell, the young girl who came to the doore wished to know who we wanted to see. Evidently we were not expected. Papa told her who we wanted to see, and she showed us to the parlor. We waited no one came; and waited no one came, still no one came, it was beginning to seem pretty awkward, "Well this is a pretty piece of business" papa exclaimed at length we heard foot steps coming down the long corridors, and Miss C.—(the lady who had invited papa) came into the room. She greeted papa very pleasantly, and they had a nice little chatt

* "Ah Holy Mary, Mother of Jesus!" CN
† "Oh God!" CN

together. Soon the lady Principal also entered the room, and she was very pleasant and agreable. She showed us to our rooms, and said she would send for us when dinner was ready. We went into our rooms, but we had nothing to do for half an hour, exept to watch the rain drops as they fell upon the window panes. At last we were called to dinner and I went down without papa as he never eats any thing in the middle of the day.

I sat at the table with the lady Principal and enjoyed very much seing all the young girls trooping into the dining room. After dinner I went around the College with the young ladies and papa stayed in his room and smoked. When it was supper time papa went down and ate supper with us and we had a very delightful supper. After supper the young ladies went to their rooms to dress for the evening, papa went to his room and I went with the Lady Principal. At length the guests began to arive, but papa still remained in his room, until called for. Papa read in the chapell. It was the first time I had ever heard him read in my life, that is in public. When he came out onto the stage I remember the people behind me exclaimed "oh how queer he is! "isn't he funny!" I thought papa was very funny although I did not think him queer. He read "A Trying Situation" and "The Golden Arm" a ghost story that he heard down South when he was a little boy. The Golden Arm papa had told me before but he had startelled me so that I did not much wish to hear it again. But I had resolved this time to be prepared and not to let myself be startled. But still papa did and very, very much, he startled the whole room full of people and they jumped as one man. The other story was also very funny and interesting and I enjoyed the evening inexpressibly much. After papa had finished reading, we all went down to the Collation in the dining room, and after that there was dancing and singing then the guests went away and papa and I went to bed.

The next morning we rose early took an early train for Hartford and reached Hartford at 1/2 past 2 o'clock. We were very glad to get back. x x x x

How charitably she treats that ghastly experience! It is a dear and lovely disposition, and a most valuable one, that can brush away indignities and discourtesies and seek and find the pleasanter features of an experience. Susy had that disposition, and it was one of the jewels of her character that had come to her straight from her mother. It is a feature that was left out of me at birth. And, at seventy, I have not yet acquired it. I did not go to Vassar College professionally, but as a guest—as a guest, and gratis. Aunt Clara (now Mrs. John B. Stanchfield) was a graduate of Vassar and it was to please her that I inflicted that journey upon Susy and myself. The invitation had come to me from both the lady mentioned by Susy and the President of the College—a sour old saint who has probably been gathered to his fathers long ago; and I hope they enjoy him; I hope they value his society. I think I can get along without it, in either end of the next world.

We arrived at the College in that soaking rain, and Susy has described, with just a suggestion of dissatisfaction, the sort of reception we got. Susy had to sit in her damp clothes half an hour while we waited in the parlor; then she was taken to a fireless room and left to wait there again, as she has stated. I do not remember that President's name, and I am sorry. He did not put in an appearance until it was time for me to step upon the platform in front of that great garden of young and lovely blossoms. He caught up with me and advanced upon the platform with me and was going to introduce me. I said in substance:

"You have allowed me to get along without your help thus far, and if you will retire from the platform I will try to do the rest without it."

I did not see him any more, but I detest his memory. Of course my resentment did not extend to the

students, and so I had an unforgettable good time talking to them. And I think they had a good time too, for
they responded "as one man," to use Susy's unimprovable phrase.

I stopped in the middle of mamma's
early history to tell about our tripp to Vassar because I was afraid I would forget
about it, now I will go on where I left off.
Some time after Miss E. Nigh died Papa
took mamma and little Langdon to Elmira
for the summer. When in Elmira Langdon
began to fail but I think mamma did not
know just what was the matter with him.
At last it was time for papa to return to
Hartford and Langdon was real sick at that
time, but still mamma decided to go with
him thinking the journey might do him
good. But after they reached Hartford he
became very sick and his trouble proved to
be diptheria. He died about a week after
mamma and papa reached Hartford. After
that mamma became very very ill, so ill that
there seemed great danger of death, but
with a great deal of good care she recovered.
Little Langdon was buried by the side of
Grandpa at Elmira, N.Y.*

* Susy rests there with them. SLC

Some months afterward mamma and papa* went to Europe and stayed for a time in Scotland and England. In Scotland mamma and papa became very well equainted with Dr. John Brown the author of "Rab and His Friends" and mett but was not so well equainted with Mr. Charles Kingsley, Mr. Henry M. Stanley, Sir Thomas Hardy (grandson of the Mr. Hardy to whom Nellson said "Kiss me Hardy" when dying on shipboard) Mr. Henry Irving, Robert Browning Sir Charles Dilke, Mr. Charles Reade Mr. Black, Lord Houghton (Muncton Milnes) Frank Buckland, Mr. Tom Hughes, Anthony Trollope, Tom Hood, son of the poet and mamma and papa were quite well equainted with Dr. Mc Donald and family, and papa met Harison Ainsworth.

Papa went to Europe to lecture and after staying in Scotland and England and making a flying tripp through Ireland, he returned home with mama.

Last winter papa was away for many months reading with Mr. G.W. Cable, and while he was gone we composed the plan of

* And Susy, who was a year old at the time. SLC

surprising him when he came home by acting Scenes from the "Prince and Pauper."* It took us a great while to commit all that was necesary but at last we were almost ready and we expected him to come home the next day on which evening we had planned to surprise him. But we received a telegram from him stating that he would reach Hartford "today at 2 o'clock." We were all dismayed for we were by no means prepared to receive him. The library was strewn with costumes which were to be tried on for the last time and we had planned a dress rehearsal over at Mr. Warners for that afternoon.

But mamma gathered the things up as quickly as possble and hustled them into the mahogany room.

Soon we heard the carriage roll over the pavement in front of the house and we all rushed to the doore. After we had partially gotten over our surprise and delight at seeing papa we all went into the library. We all sat with papa a little while and then mamma dissapeared into the mahogany room. Clara and I sat with papa a while so

* Dramatised from the book by her mother. SLC

as to prevent his being surprised of our
seemingly uncalled for disertion of him.
But soon we too had to withdraw to the mahogany room so as to help mamma sew on
bucles onto slippers and pack costumes into
a clothes basket. Papa was left all alone; Exept that one of us every once in a while
would slipp in and stay with him a little
while. Any one but papa would have wondered at mammas unwonted absence, but
papa is to absence minded, he very seldom
notices things as accurately as other people
do; although I do not believe in this instance he could have been wholly without
suspicion.* At last he went up to the billiard room and Jean went with him.
Mamma as a special favor let Jean in to this
secret on condition that she would not
breathe a whisper to any one on the subject
especially to papa and Jean had promised.
But when alone up in papa's room, it was
very hard for her not to tell papa the whole
thing. As it was she was undecided whether
to tell him or not. She did go so far as to
begin with "Its a secret papa" and then
dropping various other hints about the se-

* But I was. SLC

Jean, about 1885

cret* and she went so far that papa said afterwards that if he had beene anyone else he
should have guessed it in a minute.

At ½ past three o'clock we all started
for Mr. Warners house there to have our rehearsal Jean and the nurse went with us, so
papa was left absolutely alone.

The next day the first information that

---

* At this place in the manuscript, at the top of page 36, there is
a note, apparently in SLC's hand: "So rich in record—Jean's lack of
ability to keep a secret." CN

Margaret Warner as the Pauper, Susy as the Prince

papa got was that he was invited for the evening and he did not know that anything unusual was going to happen until he sat before the curtain.

We got through the scenes quite successfully and had some delightful dancing afterwards. After we had danced for about half an hour mamma seemed in quite a hurry to get home, so we put on our things and started for home.

When we entered the library a lady was sitting in one of the arm chairs I did not recognise her and wondered why mamma did not introduce me to her but on drawing nearer to her chair I saw it was Aunt Clara Spaulding! x x x x

Mamma told aunt Clara that we would have the "Prince and Pauper" again in a few weeks so she could see it. So it was decided that we should have it again in a few weeks. At length the time was sett and we were nearly prepared, when Frank Warner who took the "Miles Hendon" part caught a severe cold and could not play it, so papa said that he would take the part. Papa had only three days to learn the part in, but still

we were all sure that he could do it. The
scene that he acted in was the scene between Miles Hendon and the Prince, "The
Prithee pour the Water!" scene. I was the
Prince and Papa and I rehearsed together 2
or 3 times a day for the three days before
the appointed evening. Papa acted his part
beautifully and he added to the scene making it a good deal longer. He was inexpressibly funny, with his great Slouch hat and
gait! oh such a gait! Papa made the Miles
Hendon scene a splendid success and every
one was delighted with the scene and papa
too. We had great great funn with our
Prince and Pauper and I think we none of
us shall forget how imensely funny papa
was in it. He certainly could have been an
actor as well as an author.*

The other day we were all sitting when
papa told Clara and I that he would give us
an arithmetic example, he began if A byes a
horse for $100—"200" Jean interupted, the
expression of mingled surprise and submis-
sion on papa face as he turned to Jean and

---

* Susy's opinion stands now justified, and mightily reinforced,
after sixteen or seventeen years; for at dinner the other night after I
had told about (I forget what), Sir Henry Irving let fall the same
remark. *Riverdale, November 1901.* SLC

said "who is doing this example Jean?" Jean laughed and papa continued. If <u>A</u> byes a horse for $100-"200" Jean promptly interupted: papa looked perplexed and mamma went into convulsions of laughter. It was plain to us all that papa would have to change his summ to $200, so he accordingly began. "If <u>A</u> byes a horse for $200 and <u>B</u> byes a mule for $140 and they join in copartnership and trade their chreatures for a

The house at Quarry Farm, Elmira, New York.

Mark Twain in Quarry Farm study

piece of land $480 how long will it take a lame man to borrow a silk umbrella.

Papa's great care now is "Sour Mash" (the cat) and he will come way down from his studdy on the hill to see how she is getting along.

A few months after the last Prince and Pauper we started for "The Farm. The farm is aunt Susies home and where we stay in the summer, it is situated on the top of a high hill overlooking the valley of Elmira. In the winter papa sent way to Kansas for a little donkey for us to have at the farm, and when we got to the farm we were delighted to find the donky in good trimm and ready

Mark Twain in study at Quarry Farm, 1903

"Kiditchin" with unidentified children

to have us ride her. But she has proved to be
very balky, and we have to make her go by
walking in front of her with a handfull of
crackers. Papa wrote a little poem about her
which I have, and will put in here, it is
partly German partly English.

<u>Kiditchin</u>*
"O du lieb' Kiditchin,
Du bist ganz bewitchin'†
"Waw – – – he!"

* Cadichon—pronounced Kaditchin by the children. SLC
† O you dear Kiditchin,/You are totally bewitchin'. CN

"Our summer days Kiditchin
  Thour't dear from nose to britchin"
    "Waw – – – he!"

"No dought thoult get a switchin
  When for mischief thour't itchin'
    "Waw – – – he!"

"But when youre good Kiditchin
  You shall feast in James's kitchen."
    "Wah – – – he!"

"Anon lift up thy song—
  Thy noble note prolong,—
  Thou living chinese gong!"
    "Waw – – – – he! Waw – – – – he!
    Waw – – – – he!"

"Swetest donkey man ever saw."
                    Mark Twain

There are eleven cats at the farm here
now, and papa's favorite a little Tortoise
Shell kitten he has named "Sour Mash" and
a little spotted one "Famine".
    It is very to see what papa calls the cat
prosession it was formed in this way. Old
Minnie-cat headed (the mother of all the
cats), next to her came aunt Susie, then

Clara on the donkey, accompanied by a file of cats, then papa and Jean hand in hand and a file of cats brought up the rear, mamma and I made up the audience.

Our varius occupations are as follows. Papa rises about 1/2 past 7 in the morning, breakfasts at eight, writes plays tennis with Clara and me in and tries to make the donkey go in the morning does varius things and in the evening plays tennis with Clara and me and amuses Jean and the donkey.

Mamma rises about 1/4 to eight, breakfasts at eight, teaches Jean German reading from 9–10, reads German with me from 10–11—Then she reads or studdies or visits with aunt Susie for a while, and then she reads to Clara and I till lunch time things connected with English history for we hope to go to England next summer, while we sew. Then we have lunch. She studdies for about a half an hour or visits with aunt Susie, then reads to us an hour or more, then studdies write reads and rests till supper time. After supper she sits out on the porch and works till eight o'clock, from eight o'clock till bedtime she plays whist with papa, and after she has retired she reads and studdies German for a while.

Clara and I do most every thing from practicing to donkey riding and playing tag. While Jean's time is spent in asking mamma what she can have to eet.—x x x x x x

It is Jean's birth day to day.* She is 5 yrs. old Papa is away to day and he telegraphed Jean that he wished her 65 happy returns. Papa has just written something about General Grant's Getesburg speech. I will put it in here.

"General Grant."

Any one who has had the privillige of knowing General Grant personaly will recognize how justly General Beale recently out lined his great and simple and beautiful nature. Thirteen hundred years ago, as the legends of King Arthur's Round table have it, Sir Launcelot, the flower of cristian chivalry, the knight without a peer, lay dead in the castle of Joyous Yard. With a loving and longing heart, his brother the knight Sir Ector de Maris had been seeking him patiently for seven lagging years, and now he arived at this place at night fall and heard the chanting of monks over the dead. In the

* July 26, 1885. SLC

quaint and charming English of nearly 4 hundred years ago the story says,—

"And when Sir Ector heard such noise and light in the quire of Joyous Yard he alight, and put his horse from him, and came into the quire and there he saw men sing and weep. And all they knew Sir Ector but he knew not them. Then went Sir Bors unto Sir Ector and told him how there lay his brother Sir Launcelot dead: and then Sir Ector threw his shield, sword, and helm, from him; and when he beheld Sir Launcelot's visage, he fell down in a swoon: and when he awaked it were hard for any tongue to tell the doleful complaints that he made for his brother."

Then follows his tribute—a passage whose noble and simple eloquence had not its equal in English literature, until the Gettesburg speech took its lofty place beside it. The words drew a portrait 13 centuries ago; they draw its twin to day without the alteration of a syllable:—

Ah Launcelot thou were head of all christian knights! And now I dare say, thou Sir Launcelot, there thou liest, that thou were never matched of earthly knits hands;

and thou were the courtiest knight, that ever bare shield, and thou were the truest friend to thy friend that ever bestrode horse; and thou were the truest lover, of a sinful man, that ever loved woman, and thou were the kindest man that ever strake with sword; and thou were the goodliest person that ever came among press of knights; and thou were the meekest man and the gentlest that ever ate in hall among ladies, and thou were the sternest knight to thy mortal foe that ever put spear in rest."

S.L.C.

July 1885

The other day papa thought he would see how he could manage Cadichon who had been acting badly so he got onto her but papa wanted to go one way and Cadichon another, and as papa wouldn't submit Cadichon threw him off into the high grass.

About a half an hour later Jean came down onto the porch in her night gown and sat on mammas lap. I said Jean what do you think! Cadichon threw papa off into the high grass! She answerd in a very calm way "I know it" I said how do you know it? She said oh I saw it from the window." She had been in the habit of standing at the window in her night gown and crittisizing the the shotts papa and I made while playing tennis and we wondered why she did not crittisize the way papa fell from Cadichon.

Papa had just written to the editor of the Sun what he thinks about Gen. Grants burial. I will put it in here.

"General Grant's Burial."
Will the Great Captain be Removed:—
A Suggestion by Mark Twain

To the editor of the "Sun."—"Sir: The newspaper atmosphere is charged with objections to New York as the sepulchre of General Grant, and the objectors are strenuous that Washington is the right place. They offer good reasons,—good temporary reasons,—for both of these positions.

But it seems to me that temporary reasons are not meet for the occation. We need to consider posterity rather than our own generation. We should select a grave which will not merely be in the right place now, but will still be in the right place five hundred years from now.

How does Washington promise as to that?—You only have to hit it in one place to kill it. Some day the West will be numerically strong enough to remove the seat of government; her past attempts are a fair warning that when that day comes she will do it. Then the city of Washington will lose it's consequence, and pass out of the public news, and the public talk. It is quite within the possibilities that a century hence people would wonder and say, "how does it come, that our predecessors buried their great dead in this deserted place?"

"But as long as American civilization lasts New York will last. I cannot but think she has beene well and wisely chosen as the guardian of a grave which is destined to become almost the most conspicuous in the worlds history. Twenty centuries from now New York will still be New York, still a vast city, and the most notable object in it will still be the tomb and monument of General Grant.

I observe that the common and strongest objection to New York is that she is not national ground. Let us give ourselves no uneasyness about that. Wherever General Grants body lies that is national ground.

S. L. Clemens
July 27th '85

Papa says that if collera comes here he will take Sour Mash to the mountains.

The other day* Jean was taking a walk with papa and as she passed the barn she saw some little newly born baby ducks she turned to papa and said "I wonder why God gives us so much ducks as Patrick kills so many."†

Papa has gone to New York to attend Gen. Grant's funeral. And he wrote mamma that the mourning put up for President Garfield was not to be compared with that put up for Gen. Grant. He wrote that there were a great many pictures of Gen. Grant just set in a sea of black. Papa has come home to day and we were all delighted to see him. It was beautiful to hear him discribe the procession in New York in

* [At Hartford]—SLC
† "kills them so." SLC

honor of Gen. Grant. Papa's friend, Mr. Gherhardt a young american artist who made a bust of Gen. Grant has just received the privillige of making a statue of Gen. Grant, and we hope will get a part in the great New York statue.

Aug. 24. Mamma and Papa have gone to visit Mrs. Wheeler the mother of the artist Miss Dora Wheeler, at Tannersville N.Y. and they will meet there Mr. and Mrs. F. R. Stockton, Mr. and Mrs. Dean Sage, and Mrs. Mary Mapes Dodge. They are anticipating a delightful visit.

Aug. 29 Mamma and papa have returned and they have had a delightful visit. Mr. Stockton was down in Virginia and could not reach Tannersville in time so they did not see him and Mrs. Dodge was ill and couldn't go to Tannersville. But Mrs. General Custor was there and mamma said that she was a very attractive sweet appearing woman.

Sour Mash is a constant source of anxiety, care and pleasure to papa.

Mamma has given me a very pleasant little news paper scrap about papa, to copy. I will put it in here.—

"I saw a rather disparaging paragraph the other day, that recalled an incident of the Grant obsequies. I was at the Fifth Avenue Hotel at night, when the large halls were crowded with a mob of Americans celebrites. As we were looking toward the great staircase I saw James Redpath throw a kiss to a man going up, who turned with a friendly smile and tossed back a similar salutation. "Who is that?" I asked "That"— said Mr. Redpath "is the man who made death easy for Gen. Grant." "Who—Shady or Douglas?"* "No" said our friend "it is Mr. Clemens—Mark Twain. If it had not been for him Grant's death bed would have been haunted by the fear of poverty for his wife and children. "I wish he added I could tell all I know about Mark's noble and knightly generosity. But I learned only under the seal of confidence. Mark deliberately alows men who would have driven a hard bargain with Grant to malign him when he could crush them by a simple statement. But I tell you the time will come when, if the newspaper reports of this day

* Physicians. SLC

are read, people will ask why Mark Twain was not given the chief place in the procession. He did more than any living man to make Grant die without dread or regret. Mark is a better man than he is an author and there is no dought I guess that he is great with his pen." I recall this remark as I saw Mark sneeringly referred to the other day.

Sep. 9th '85

Mamma is teaching Jean a little natural history and is making a little collection of insects for her. But mamma does not allow Jean to kill any insects she only colects those insects that are found dead. Mamma has told us all, particularly Jean, to bring her all the little dead insects that she finds. The other day as we were all sitting at supper Jean broke into the room and ran triumfantly up to mamma and presented her with a plate full of dead flies. Mamma thanked Jean very enthusiastically although she with difficulty concealed her amusement. Just then Sour Mash entered the room and Jean believing her hungry asked mamma for permission to give her the flies. Mamma laughingly consented and the flow- ers* almost immediately dissapeared.

Sep. 10th '85

The other evening Clara and I brought down our new soap bubble water and we all blew soap bubbles. Papa blew his soap bub- bles and filled them with smoke and as the light shone on theire colors they look very beautiful opaline. Papa would hold them and then let us catch them in our hand and they felt delightful to the touch the mixture of the smoke and water had singularly pleasant effect.

Nov. 29th '85

Papa was fifty years old last Nov.† and among his numerous presents The Critick sent him a delightful notice of his semicen- tennial; containing a poem to him by Dr. Holms a paragraph from Mr. F. R. Stock- ton, one from Mr. C. D. Warner, and one from Mr. J. C. Harris (Uncle Remus).

Papa was very much pleased and so

---

* "Flies?" In his appetites Sour Mash was without sentiment or prejudice. SLC

† A strange slip of the pen. Clemens was fifty the next day. CN

were we all. I will put the poem and paragraphs in here.

The Critic*
Mark Twains semi-Centenial*

Mark Twain's Semi-Centennial.

Mark Twain will be half-a-hundred years old on Monday: Within the past half-century he has done more than any other man to lengthen the lives of his contemporaries by making them merrier, and it looks as if he were going to do even more good in this way within the next fifty years than in those just ended. We print below a few letters of condolence from writers whose pens, like his, have increased 'the stock of harmless pleasures,' and whom we have reminded of the approach of Mr. Clemens's first semi-centennial.

My Dear Mr. Clemens:

In your first half-century you have made the world laugh more than any other man. May you repeat the whole performance and 'mark twain!'
Yours very truly,
Charlottesville, Va.   Frank R. Stockton

My Dear Neighbor:

You may think it an easy thing to be fifty years old, but you will find it not so easy to stay there, and your next fifty years will slip away much faster than those just accomplished. After all, half a century is not much, and I wouldn't throw it up to you now, only for the chance of saying that

* In Susy's hand. Then follow clippings pasted into her book.
CN

few living men have crowded so much into that space as you, and few have done so much for the entertainment and good fellowship of the world. And I am glad to see that you wear your years as lightly as your more abundant honors. Having successfully turned this corner, I hope that we shall continue to be near neighbors and grow young together. Ever your friend,

Chas. Dudley Warner

To Mark Twain

(ON HIS FIFTIETH BIRTHDAY)

Ah Clemens, when I saw thee last,—
We both of us were younger,—
How fondly mumbling o'er the past
Is Memory's toothless hunger!

So fifty years have fled, they say,
Since first you took to drinking,—
I mean in Nature's milky way,—
Of course no ill I'm thinking.

But while on life's uneven road
Your track you've been pursuing,
What fountains from your wit have flowed—
What drinks you have been brewing!

I know whence all your magic came,—
Your secret I've discovered,—
The source that fed your inward flame—
The dreams that round you hovered:

Before you learned to bite or munch
Still kicking in your cradle,
The Muses mixed a bowl of punch
And Hebe seized the ladle.

PAPA

Dear babe, whose fiftieth year to-day
  Your ripe half-century rounded,
Your books the precious draught betray
  The laughing Nine compounded.

So mixed the sweet, the sharp, the strong,
  Each finds its faults amended,
The virtues that to each belong
  In happier union blended.

And what the flavor can surpass
  Of sugar, spirit, lemons?
So while one health fills every glass
  Mark Twain for Baby Clemens!

Nov. 23rd, 1885.   Oliver Wendell Holmes

To the Editors of *The Critic:*

There must be some joke about this matter, or else fifty years are not as burdensome as they were in the days when men were narrow-minded and lacked humor—that is to say, when there was no Mark Twain to add salt to youth and to season old age. In those days a man at fifty was conceded to be old. If he had as many enemies as he had grandchildren it was thought that he had lived a successful life. Now Mark Twain has no grandchildren, and his enemies are only among those who do not know how to enjoy the humor that is inseparable from genuine human nature.

I saw Mr. Twain not so very long ago piloting a steamboat up and down the Mississippi River in front of New Orleans, and his hand was strong and his eye keen. Somewhat later I heard him discussing a tough German sentence with Little Jean—a discussion in which the toddling child probably had the best of it,—but his mind was clear, and he was bubbling over with good humor. I have seen him elsewhere and under other circumstances, but the fact that he was bordering on fifty years never occurred to me.

And yet I am glad that he is fifty years old. He has earned the right to grow old and mellow. He has put his youth in his books, and there it is perennial. His last book is better than his first, and there his youth is renewed and revived. I know that some of the professional critics will not agree with me, but there is not in our fictive literature a more wholesome book than 'Huckleberry Finn.' It is history, it is romance, it is life. Here we behold human character stripped of all tiresome details; we see people growing and living; we laugh at their humor, share their griefs; and, in the midst of it all, behold we are taught the lesson of honesty, justice and mercy.

But this is somewhat apart from my purpose; it was my desire simply to join *The Critic* in honoring the fiftieth anniversary of an author who has had the genius to be original, and the courage to give a distinctively American flavor to everything he has ever written.

Joel Chandler Harris

Hartford Daily Courant
Mark Twain's Home

A few steps only from Mrs. Stowe's brings you to Mr. Clemens's house, and still fewer, if you take the short-cut through the lawns and shrubbery, by which brief transit you pass from old New England to modern America—from the plain quarters of ethical fiction to the luxurious abode of the most western of humorists. It is not difficult to trace, however, the essential kinship between Sam Lawson of *Oldtown Folks* and the equally quaint and shrewd but more expansive drollery of Mark Twain; and, on the other hand, those who see much of this author in private discover in him a fund of serious reflection and of keen observation upon many sub-

The dining room, Hartford house

jects that gives him another element in common with his neighbor. The literary group in this neighborhood do not seem to fancy giving names to their houses; they are content with the arithmetical designation. "No, my house has not got any name," said Mr. Clemens, in answer to a question. "It has a number, but I have never been able to remember what it is." No number, in fact, appears on gate or door; but the chances are that if a stranger were to step into any shop on the business streets he could at once obtain an accurate direction to the spot. And a charming haunt it is, with its wide hall, finished in dark wood under a panelled ceiling, and full of easy-chairs, rugs, cushions, and carved furniture that instantly invite the guest to lounge in front of the big fire-place. But it is a house made for hospitality, and one cannot stop at that point. Over the fire-place, through a large plate-glass suggesting Alice's Adventures, a glimpse is had of the drawing-room, luminous with white and silver and pale blue; and on another side, between a broad flight of stairs and a chiselled Ginevra chest drawn against the wall, the always open library door attracts one's steps. There is more dark woodwork in the library, including a very elaborate panel rising above the mantel to the ceiling. This was brought from abroad, and in other portions of the house are other pieces representing the spoils of European tours: one in particular I recall, covered with garlands and with plump cherubs that spring forth in plastic rotundity, and clamber along the edges. But it adds to the pleasurableness of the home that all the cherubs in it are not carved. A genial atmosphere, too, pervades the house, which is warmed by wood fires, a furnace, and the author's immense circulation. One would, naturally, in such a place expect to find some perfection of a study, a literary work-room, and that has indeed been provided, but the unconventional genius of the author could not reconcile itself to a surrounding the charms of which distracted his attention. The study remains, its deep window giving a seductive outlook above the library, but Mr. Clemens goes elsewhere. Pointing to a large divan extending along the two sides of a right-angled corner, "That was a good idea," he said, "which I got from something I saw in a Syrian monastery; but I found it was much more comfortable to lie there and smoke than to stay at my desk. And then these windows —I was constantly getting up to look at the view; and when one of our beautiful heavy snow-falls came in winter, I couldn't do anything at all except gaze at it." So he has moved still higher up-stairs into the billiard-room, and there writes at a table placed in such wise that he can see nothing but the wall in front of him and a couple of shelves of books. Before adopting this expedient he had tried a room which he caused to be fitted up with plain pine sheathing on the upper floor of his stable; but that had serious disadvantages, and even the billiard-room failing to meet the requirements in some emergencies, he has latterly resorted to hiring an office in a commercial building in the heart of the city.

"About four months in the year," said he, "is the time when I expect to do my work, during the summer vacation, when I am off on the farm at Elmira." "Yes," he continued, when I expressed surprise, "I can write better in hot weather. And, besides, I must be free from all other interests and occupations. I find it necessary, when I have begun anything, to keep steadily at it, without changing my surroundings. To take up the train of ideas after each day's writing I must be in the same place that I began it in, or else it becomes very difficult."

But nothing, apparently, interrupts the spontaneous flow of his humor in daily life. It is the same in kind with that of his books, though incidental and less elaborate. It is unpremeditated, and always unexpected. He never takes what may be termed the obvious and conventional witty view, yet neither is there any straining for a new form of jest: the novelty comes of itself. Moreover, unlike certain wits whose quality is genuine, but whose reputation becomes a burden to them, he appears to be indifferent whether he ever cracks another joke, and thus lulls his companions into a delusive security, only to take them unawares with some new and telling shot. There is less exaggeration in what he says than in what he writes; but the essence of his fun lies in that same grave assumption of absurdities as solid and reasonable facts with which we are familiar in his works. By a reverse process, when talking to a serious point, or narrating some experience not especially ludicrous in itself, there is a lingering suspicion of humorous possibilities in his manner, which, assisted by the slow, emphatic, natural drawl of his speech, leads one to accept actual facts of a prosaic kind as delicious absurdities. In fine, it is a sort of wizardry that he exercises in conversation, stimulating the hearer by its quick mutations of drolling and earnest.—*George Parsons Lathrop, in Harper's Magazine for October.*

[Here Susy goes back a year. SLC]

Dec. <u>1884.</u> Last winter when papa was away reading he wrote me a good many letters which I have kept and will put in here. The first one is written in German.

It is evident that Susy respected my intention—which was good—but my German must have amused her. I will not apologize for its quality, since she was content to let it go unchallenged. SLC

Grand Rapids Mich.
Dec. 14 1884.

Mein Liebes Töchterchen,

Wie geht es jetzt mit der Cleveland und der Buffalo Bill? Errinerst du dich an die Bergziegen, oder Bergschäfe die wir bei der austellung Buffalo Bills zu Elmira gesehen haben? Nun die arme Thiere sind neulich dur Schiffsbauch* veloren. Diese umfall ist

* [bruck]—SLC

auf der Mississippi vorgenkommen. Der
Dampfboot an einen versteckten Fels zer-
stört wurde, und obgleich Buffalo Bill und
seine Indianer und andere Thierein gerettet
ward, die Ziegen stürtzte sich gleich ins
Wasser und man sah sie noch nie wieder.
Auch ein oder vieleicht zwei von den Buf-
falonen ertrunken wurden. Dass macht
mirs Herz so schwer dass ich nicht mehr
schreiben kann.

Schreib an mich wieder und noch
wieder meine liebling.

Papa

P.S. Meine herzlichsten grüssen an
deine Grossmama.

[Translation]

[My dear little daughter,

How are Cleveland and Buffalo Bill now? Do you remember the mountain sheep we saw at the Buffalo Bill exhibition in Elmira? The poor animals were recently lost in a
shipbelly.* This accident occurred on the Mississippi. The
steamboat broke up on a hidden rock, and although Buffalo
Bill and his Indians, and other animals, were saved, the goats
immediately plunged into the water and were never seen
again. Also, one or perhaps two of the buffalo were drowned.
That makes me so heavy-hearted that I can't write any more.

Write to me again and again, my darling.

Papa

P.S. My warmest greetings to your grandmother.]

* [wreck]—SLC

Utika, Dec. 1884.

Susie, my dear, I have been intending to
write you and Ben* for a long time, but
have been too busy. Nach meinen
Vorlesung in Ithaka ging ich in der Bier la-
ger und fand ungefähr fierzig Studenten
von Cornell Universität dort gesammelt;
und sie machten mich herzlich will durch
heftig jüchzend und platchen in die Hände.
Dann Sangen Sie viele Prachtvolle
Gesänge, mit solo und donnerhaften Chor.
Ich habe dort geblieben bis nach Mit-
ternacht, dann machte ich ihnen eine hub-
sche Redan, und erzählte zwei kommische
Geschitern, die waren mit grossen Beifal
erhielt. Nachdem fuhr ich nach Hause und
bald ins Bett gegangen wurde.

I love you sweetheart goodbye

Papa

[Translation]
[After my lecture in Ithaca I went to the beer hall and found
about forty students from Cornell University gathered there;
and they welcomed me heartily with loud cheers and clap-
ping. Then they sang many splendid songs, with a solo and

---

* When Jean was a little thing Clara and I taught her to call us
Guck and Ben, and papa thought "Ben" so appropriate a name for
Clara, that he still calls her that.—Susy

thunderous chorus. I stayed there until after midnight, then made a nice speech and told two funny stories, which were received with much applause. Afterwards I drove home and soon went to bed.]

The following letter was written not long after "Huckleberry Finn" came out, it was an answer to a letter I wrote papa telling him how much Margaret Warner (a friend of mine) and I had enjoyed reading the book together, and how much we admired it.

St Paul Jan 23/85

Susie dear,

I am glad you and Daisy had such a good time over Huck Finn. I wish I had another book like it ready for you.

Some young ladis school teachers—called on Mr. Cable and me yesterday afternoon, and they wanted to see my family and I showed them the picture and they were very complimentary about the group, but they said they thought Jean must be a rascal. So she is; Jean is a very attractive rascal and a very good rascal too.

The thermometer has been ridiculus for fully ten days now away down below zero allday and all night long and this in a country where the only heating apparatus known is an air tight stove. Dreadful things they are. My windows yesterday comanded a principal Street, but during the entire day I did not see a woman or a girl out of doors. Only men ventured out and very few of those. Yet at night the opera house was full of people come out partly to hear us and partly to get their noses frozen off I suppose.

I am very sorry to hear that Miss Corey and Miss Foote are sick. I hope you and mamma and the rest of you will manage to make out with colds, and not go any further with that sort of thing. Your loving Papa.

Indianapolis Feb. 8/85

Susie dear,

When I get home, you must take my Morte Arthur and read it It is the quaintest and sweetest of all books. And is full of the absolute English of 400 years ago. For instance here is a paragraph which I will quot from memory. And you too may learn it by heart for its worth it. There are only two other things in our language comparable to it for tender eloquence and simplicity, one is Mr. Lincolns Gettysburg speech, and the other has for the moment escaped my memory.————The paragraph just referred to is given a little further back under heading "Gen. Grant." "There isnt that beautiful? In this book one finds out where Tennyson got the quaint and pretty phrases which he uses in The "Idols of the king" "Lightly" and "Wave" and the rest. Yes you must read it when I come sweetheart. Kiss mamma for me; and Ben and Jean.

Papa

Chicago Feb. 3/85.

Sweetheart,

Mamma has sent me your composition, and I am very greatly pleased with it, and very much obliged to mamma for sending it. I ment to return it to mamma, but sealed my letter previously. So I'll get you to do it for me.

It appears that the violin is becoming quite the fashion among girls. One of Gen. Fairchilde's daughters plays that instrument I didn't see the girls exept the one that was a baby when we knew them in Paris. They were away on a visit. It is said that one of them is very beautiful.

In this hotel (the Grand Pacific) there is a colored youth who stands near the great dining room, and takes the hats off the gentlemen as they pass into dinner and sets them away. The people come in Shoals and sometimes he has his arms full of hats and is kept moving in a most lively way. Yet he remembers every hat, and when these people come crowding out, an hour, or an hour and a half later he hands to each gentlemen his hat and never makes any mistake. I have watched him to see how he did it but I couldn't see that he more than merely glanced at his man if he even did that much. I have tried a couple of times to make him believe he was giving me the wrong hat, but it didn't persuade him in the least. He intimated that I might be in doubt, but that he knew.

Goodbye honey

Papa

Chicago Jan./85

Susie dear, Your letter was a great pleasure to me. I am glad you like the new book; and your discription of its effect on Daisy is all that the most exacting and most praise-hungry author could desire. And by the way this reminds me to appoint you to write me two or three times a week in mamma's place; and when you write she must <u>not</u> write. What I am after is to save <u>her</u>. She writes me when she aught to be resting herself after the heavy fatigues of the day. It is wrong. It must be stopped. You must stop it.

When it is your day to write and you have been prevented, see to it that the day passes without a letter, <u>she</u> must not write a line. Goodbye sweetheart

Papa

Toronto Feb. 15/85

Susie dear, it was a good letter you wrote me, and so was Clara's I don't think that either of you have ever written better ones.

I went toboganing yesterday and it was indiscribeable fun. It was at a girls' college in the country. The whole college—51 girls, were at the lecture the night before, and I came down off the platform at the close, and went down the aisle and overtook them and said I had come down to introduce myself, because I was a stranger, and didn't know

any body and was pretty lonesome. And so
we had a hand shake all around, and the
lady principal said she would send a sleigh
for us in the morning if we would come out
to the college. I said we would do that with
pleasure. So I went home and shaved. For I
didn't want to have to get up still earlier in
order to do that; and next morning we
drove out through the loveliest winter landscape that ever was.

Brilliant sunshine, deep snow everywhere, with a shining crust on it—not flat
but just a far reaching white ocean, laid in
long smoothe swells like the sea when a
calm is coming on after a storm, and every
where near and far were island groves of
forest trees. And farther and farther away
was a receding panorama of hills and forests
dimmed by a haze so soft and rich and
dainty and spiritual, that it made all objects
seem the unreal creatures of a dream, and
the whole a vision of a poets paradise, a
veiled hushed holy land of the imagination.

You shall see it some day.

Ich küsse dich mein liebchen*

Papa

* [I kiss you my darling]—CN

Susy as the Prince, Margaret Warner as the Pauper (probably the second production)

Feb. 6th '86.

We have just had our third "Prince and Pauper" and we have had more fun acting it than ever before, the programme was the same exept that Papa lengthened the "Lady Jane Grey Scene" in which Clara was the Lady Jane Grey. He also added a little to the interview between the prince and pauper, by putting in a little scene behind the scenes to represent their talking while changing clothes. It was as follows:*

Behind Scenes

Prince.   Oh wait! I did not notice! thoust got <u>that</u> all <u>wrong</u>, that part goes behind. Wait, let me help thee <u>truss</u> <u>the</u> <u>points</u>. There now.

Pauper.   Ah good your worship I did never truss a point In all my life before. 'Tis by the grace of God alone that my rags hang together.

Prince.   Wait, again wait! You see this goes this way, then this goes in

* And to give time for some changes in front. SLC

Clara as Lady Jane Grey

here, then one turns this back so and brings the other forward. There now it'll do.

Pauper. Ah good your worship, thou hast not disposed <u>that</u> rag to it's just advantage, prithee let me give it the touch, that is familiar to it.

Prince. Ah thanks, thanks, here I dont quite understand how this relic—ah good very good thanks, oh wait the sword belongeth on thy other side, so that's right. Come.

(they go onto stage)

The addition to the Lady Jane Grey
    scence was this.

(Pauper sitting despondently)
(enter page)

Page. The lady Jane Grey
    (Exit)
(Enter lady Jane Grey bows low)

Pauper. Oh prithee let me, out!

Lady Jane. (Surprised—alittle ruffled—with distant politeness) Let thee out! My lord since when must the prince of Wales sue to common clay for leave, to leave his room when he would, you jest my lord! and I? I do not <u>like</u> it.

Pauper.　(distressed) Oh dear lady <u>I</u> am not the prince of Wales!

Lady Jane.　(still piqued and sarcastic) Indeed! perhaps thou art Ananias or Sophyra in Sooth with practice your grace might serve for both. My lord. (another toss)

Pauper.　(distressed) Oh lady <u>do</u> not be cruel!

Lady Jane.　Cruel? I cruel! I left mine amusement to come and help thee with thy greeck.

Pauper.　Greeck? Oh dear lady I know no Greeck.

Lady Jane.　Aside. How strangely he acts. I grow afraid of him saith he knoweth no Greeck, and how strange it is that he should say that for its true! (suddenly and with terrified conviction) his minds disordered

Pauper.　(stepping nearer appealingly) Oh gracious lady—

Lady Jane.　(interupting and shooing off

                              with her hand) Donot touch
                              me! (here insert old scene
                              given in book) Oh what aileth
                              thee my lord?

Pauper.   Oh be merciful thou, in sooth
                              I am no lord, but only poor,
                              Tom Canty of Offal Court in
                              the City prithee let me see the
                              prince and he will of his grace
                              restore me to my rags and let
                              me hence unhurt Oh be thou
                              merciful and save me! [Falls on
                              his knees. SLC]

Lady Jane.   Oh my lord! On thy knees and
                              to me!
                              (Exit in a frightened way)

We produced the Prince and Pauper a number of
times. These were great occasions in the household.
Preparations were begun a week in advance of the performance; the ordinary home-traffic was obstructed, interrupted, disordered, and sometimes even paralysed
for a while, for the play was the one important interest
for the time being, and every other thing had to give
way to it. With the actors, part-studying went on constantly, and rehearsals were frequent; the non-actors
were similarly busy, planning and perfecting the arrangements, overhauling and renovating the costumes,
and so forth. The final day was particularly full. On
that day the auditorium (the library and dining-room

which opened together, with folding doors) was stripped for action, cleaned, dusted, and furnished with eighty-four chairs; the stage was brought from the stable and placed against the conservatory at the end of the library, and its equipment of scenery and curtains set up; the green-room (mahogany room) was cleared of superfluities and their places filled with costumes and matters connected with stage "business;" the piano in the drawing-room was tuned up for the marches and processions; then in the afternoon there was a dress rehearsal by the full strength of the company.

It was a day of consuming excitement and exhausting but willing and joyous labor, and not a member of the family nor any servant in house or stable had an idle moment. Susy and her troupe were in a happy heaven of excitement all the day, and all the busy household moved and toiled in an atmosphere that was electric with their enthusiasms.

We dined as we could—probably with a neighbor—and by a quarter to eight in the evening the hickory fire in the hall was pouring in sheets of flame up the chimney, the house was in a drench of gas-light from the ground floor up, the guests were arriving, and there was a babel of hearty greetings, with not a voice in it that was not old and familiar and affectionate; and when the curtain went up we looked out from the stage upon none but faces that were dear to us, none but faces that were lit up with welcome for us.

I think we were a competent company, and I know we played our parts with tremendous earnestness, and that if there was a member who did not live the character he represented,—and vividly live it, and lose the consciousness of his own personality in it,—it was I, and not any younger member. Susy was the Prince, Daisy Warner was the Pauper, Clara was Lady Jane Grey; the minor characters by children of the neighborhood. I have seen nothing prettier or more moving than the acting of these little creatures. The fire they put into it was real, not a fiction of the stage. There were no dull places in the piece; it swept along, full charged with interest and animation, from the beginning to the end. Then came the grand climax—the Coronation; with its impressivenesses, its waiting suspenses, its threatened defeats and miscarriages, its bursts of passion breaking the line here and there, its triumphant close, with martial music and processions. It was our great scene, the pride and joy of the children, and into it they put their whole hearts.

Many of the pictures in the piece stand out vividly in my memory yet. In the added part (copied by Susy in the Biography) I can see little Clara doing her stately dignities and "distant politeness," and hear her say, with a fine disdain which was comical because it was so serious—

"My lord, since when must the *Prince of Wales* sue to common clay for leave to leave his room when he would?" A pause—with a gathering sense of injury. "You jest, my lord. And I (with a toss of the head) "I do not *like* it!"

And I can see Daisy (as Tom Canty in the royal robes) when she stamps her foot, and puts out her hand, and says—

"On your peril! Touch him not, he is the King!"

I can see Susy (as the restored King) protecting

Tom Canty, and hear her saying, with the security of assured authority and in a gentle voice pathetically reminiscent of late sadnesses and hardships—

"I will not have it so. But for him I had not got my crown again—none shall lay a hand upon him to harm him." And I can see her lift her eyes reproachfully upon the Lord Protector, and hear her voice harden as she proceeds with the rest of the speech. I can see the scene where she protects me when I sit down in the royal presence—"Touch him not, it is his right!" and I can see her face and hear her voice in that speech which she loved the best of all—the "curtain" speech—the one spoken over the kneeling Pauper—which closed the piece and ended with the words,

"He hath the Throne's protection, he hath the crown's support, he shall be known and called by the honorable title of the King's Ward."

Susy begins the Biography with the remark, "We are a very happy family." It was true.

I am now approaching some stories which I told Jean, and which Susy has put into the Biography—not because she thought them good, but because the dilapidations they suffered in Jean's reproductions of them amused her. In truth I find them battered and dismembered beyond recognition. Still, they shall stand, just as Susy set them down; their vacancies and incoherences—together with Jean's successes in leaving out the point every time there happened to be one—pleased her, and that is sufficient. It is probable that Jean furnished the texts for the stories herself—it was her custom, and was fraught with difficulties for me. Once her text was,

"Tell a story about a bawgunstructor (boa constrictor) and a burglar."* I managed it, but it strained me. It seems a sort of pity that that one does not appear here. After Jean's editing, it would have been a satisfactory wreck to Susy, no doubt, and not destitute of picturesquenesses.

Of the near and dear friends who sat before our stage and applauded our Prince and Pauper, many are gone: among them Henry Robinson, Miss Hamersley, Edward M. Bunce, Charles Dudley Warner, but to the roll-call of the actors, all can still answer to their names —save two. (Fanny Freese)

Feb. 7th 86. Jean who is just five† years old, has learned the part of the lady Jane Grey by hearing us rehearse, and she can act it quite well making up for the words she cant get straight, by adding great emphasies to the ones she knows.

Feb. 7th I overheard papa telling Jean a story this morning, it amused me very much it was a story of Such great variety, and indeed papa has practise in telling stories of variety as Jean is achild of variety and original ideas, and papa is too, (I mean such a man) so half of the story he devotes

---

* In the Foreword, Clemens credits Clara with asking him to invent this tale. CN
† and a half. SLC

to his own fancy, (if Jean allows) the other half to Jeans; I heard only a part of the story this morning, so I asked Jean to tell it to me afterwards so she did, and here it is as she gives it.

"Well once there was a register who went out walking. He saw a school-house and he went into the school-house; he saw the big children pushed away little children in the cold part of the room. He went in a corner and warmed the little childern and as soon as the little childern said it felt so warm, the big childern came and pushed them away* and then one of the big boys said, he would put in his finger and try to open it and snapp closed the register tighter with his finger in. Then the little children had the stove. Then the boy that was pinched howled and cryed so that the other big children couldn't stay in the school house. So they went out and looked to see where that heatness came from, they thought it came from the sun or from the ground and they couldnt see. Then they went and borrowed quite a few baloons and went up in the air, and they went up higher

* when the rig closed—SLC

and higher and higher, and higher and they let out a bird, the children put out ahed were frozen when the bird didn't know where he was, and he went among the clouds, and pretty soon he came back sailing back again and they sailed and sailed and sailed and went over oceans and seas and ships and pretty soon they landed in Africa. Quite a few plain people and a few indians came, and some lions and tigers, and the lions nibbled at the frozen children, and couldnt bite them. Then a man came and said they were missionarys on the half shell and they must be thawed out. So they thawed them out, and pretty soon they got growed up to women and men, and were very good missionarys and converted many, and alast wer eaten at a barbecue. Jean, who is very fond of animals, demands strictly animal stories from papa, for which I am very sorry, as I think his other stories are better. Here is another story, of papa's, told to me by Jean.

A Tiger in the Jungle.

Once there was a tiger lying in a jungle on a very hot day, he heard a cow infront of

him "Moo,—"Moo" Moo" He got up and
said and said he would have a real nice
breakfast. But he couldn't catch the cow
and he heard a little calf, so he stopped trying to catch the cow and ran after the calf,
pretty soon he heard a cat "meaw"—"meau,
still nearer him than the calf, so he chased
the cat, then he heard a dog,—"Bow, wow,"
so he ran after the dog then he heard a
rooster "Cuck-adoodle doo,"—then he ran
after the rooster, round, and round, and
round, the rooster seemed nearer, and
nearer, but still he couldn't get it, at last he
fell down dead, from tiredness. He had
been running after his own tail.

This story was told in the same way as
the two preceeding ones.

The Donkey What Could Talk

Once there was a donkey and he went
out walking. And he saw some children and
he wondered why those children had books
under their arms, And he thought he would
go with them to see what they did. And he
went into the School-house with them and
they showed him their books. But he

couldn't understand the words in the books. So one evening moonshine he thought he would go to the school-house, and eat some of the books. He went and ate, German books, and English books, and French books and all kinds of books, and had a great deal of stomach ache afterwards. And when the children came home they wondered where their books were, and they couldn't see where the books were, they couldnt see Then the childrern said, "Why this donkey must have eaten our books. But the donkey said he hadn't touched books. Then the school-teacher came home and the children said that this donkey could talk. And the school-teacher wanted to hear him. So the children called him, and he came and spoke to them, and as soon as the people saw, heard this wonderful donkey talk, they immediately asked him to belong to their church. So he did. And when the choir sang, he sang with it, but he was not satisfied to sing in company with others, fearing his voice, might not be distinctly enough heard. So he asked for permission to sing alone in place of the choir so his request was granted him, and he sang regulary after that, every Sunday. At last people got so much interested in him that he was ellected to be Member of Congress, which honor he also accepted; and he was the first donkey that ever was Member of Congress. And finally he ran for President and so he was the learnedest donkey that ever was.———

Feb. 12 '86

Mamma and I have both been very much troubled of late because papa, since he has been publishing Gen. Grant's book, has seemed to forget his own books and work entirely, and the other evening as papa and I were promonading up and down the library he told me that he didn't expect to write but one more book, and then he was ready to give up work altogether, die or do anything, he said that he had written more than he had ever expected to, and the only book that he had been pertickularly anxious to write was one locked up in the safe down stairs, not yet published.*

But this intended future of course will never do, and although papa usualy holds to his own opinions and intents with outsid-

* It is there yet. SLC The manuscript was "Captain Storm-field's Visit to Heaven." CN

ers, when mamma realy desires anything and says that it must be, papa allways gives up his plans (at least so far) and does as she says (and she is usually right, if she dissagrees with him at all). It was because he knew his great tendency to being convinced by her, that he published without her knowledge that article in the "Christian Union" concerning the government of children. So judging from the proofs of past years, I think that we will be able to persuade papa to go back to work as before, and not leave off writing with the end of his next Story. Mamma says that she sometimes feels, and I do too, that she would rather have papa depend on his writing for a living, than to have him think of giving it up.

Ever since papa and mamma were married, papa has written his books and then taken them to mamma in manuscript and she has expergated them. Papa read "Hucleberry Finn" to us in manuscript just before it came out, and then he would leave parts of it with mamma to expergate, while he went off up to the study to work, and sometimes Clara and I would be sitting with mamma while she was looking the manuscript over and I remember so well, with what pangs of regret we used to see her turn down the leaves of the pages which meant, that some delightfully dreadful part must be scratched out. And I remember one part pertickularly which was perfectly fascinating it was dreadful, that Clara and I used to delight in, and oh with what dispare we saw mamma turn down the leaf on which it was written, we thought the book would be almost spoiled without it. But after it was published we changed our minds. We gradually came to feel as mamma did.

It would be a pity to replace the vivacity and quaintness and felicity of Susy's innocent free spelling with the dull and petrified uniformities of the spelling-book. Nearly all the grimness is taken out of the "expergating" of my books, by the subtle mollification accidentally infused into the word by Susy's modification of the spelling of it.

I remember the special case mentioned by Susy, and can see the group yet—two-thirds of it pleading for the life of the culprit sentence that was so fascinatingly dreadful and the other third of it patiently explaining why the court could not grant the prayer of the pleaders; but I do not remember what the condemned phrase was. It had much company, and they all went to the gallows; but it is possible that that specially dreadful one which gave those little people so much delight was cunningly devised and put into the book for just that function, and not with any hope or expectation that it would get by the expergator alive. It is possible, for I had that custom, and have it yet.

Feb. 12, '86

Papa has long wanted us to have an international copywright in this country, so two or three weeks ago, he went to Washington to see what he could do to influence the government in favor of one. Here is a description of the hearing of the Senate that he attended Jan. 30 '86.

The Outlook for International Copyright.

Washington, January 30.—It is the impression of those who have followed the hearing in international copyright that the Senate Committee on Patents will report favorably the bill with the "printers' amendment," which is advocated by General Hawley, by Senator Chase, by Mr. Clemens, and other publishers who are also authors, and is accepted by the representative of the Typographical Union, which, as the agent of that Union somewhat grandiloquently told the Committee, through its affiliation with the Knights of Labor, speaks for from 4,000,000 to 5,000,000 people. Although it was clearly demonstrated to the Committee by Mr. Lowell and others that the American author is the only laborer who is obliged to compete with those who are not paid anything, the influence of the book manufacturers, and of labor unions, and of the various protected interests, is so strong in Congress that those who boast that they are "practical legislators" will not support a bill solely on the ground that, as Mr. Lowell put it, "it is a measure of morality and justice." It is not, however, measures of morality and justice that can control the most votes. Mr. Clemens, in his humorous way, during the hearing said a very practical thing, in accordance with which the Committee is very likely to act. He said that while the American author has a great interest in American books, there are a great many others who are interested in book-making in its various forms, and the "other fellows" are the larger part.

Jean and Papa were walking out past the barn the other day when Jean saw some little ducks, she exclaimed as she perceived them "I dont see why God gives us so much ducks when Patrick kills so many!"

Papa has written a new version* of "There is a happy land" itis—

"There is a happy land
     Far, far away,
  Where they have ham and eggs,
     Three times a day,
  Oh dont those boarders yell
     When they hear the dinner-bell,
  They give that land-lord rats
     Three times aday.

Feb. 22.
     Yesterday evening papa read to us the

* No, it was Billy Rice's new version. SLC. Got it at his "nig-ger-show." SLC

beginning of his new book, in manuscript, and we enjoyed it very much, it was founded on a New Englanders visit to England in the time of King Arthur and his round table.—

Feb. 24. Sunday.

Clara's reputation as a baby was always a fine one, mine exactly the contrary. One often related story conscerning her braveness as a baby and her own oppinion of this quality of her, is this. Clara and I often got slivers in ours hands and when mamma took them out with a much dreaded needle, Clara was always very brave, and I very cowardly. One day Clara got one of these slivers in her hand, a very bad one, and while mamma was taking it out, Clara stood perfectly still without even wincing; I saw how brave she was and turning to mamma said "Mamma isn't she a brave little thing! presently mamma had to give the little hand quite a dig with the needle and noticing how perfectly quiet Clara was about it she exclaimed, Why Clara! You <u>are</u> a brave little thing! Clara responded "No bodys braver but God!"

Clara (no date)

Feb. 27 '86

Last summer while we were in Elmira an article came out in the "Christian Union" by name "What ought he have done" treating of the government of children, or rather giving an account of a fathers battle with his little baby boy, by the mother of the child and put in the form of a question as to whether the father disciplined the child corectly or not, different people wrote their opinions of the fathers behavior, and told what they thought he should have done. Mamma had long known how to discipline children, for in fact the bringing up of children had been one of her specialties for many years. She had a great many theorys, but one of them was that if a child was big enough to be nauty, it was big enough to be whipped and here we all agreed with her. I remember one morning when Dr. _____ came up to the farm he had a long discussion with mamma, upon the following topic. Mamma gave this as illustrative of one important rule for punishing a child. She said we will suppose the boy has thrown a handkerchief onto the floor. I tell him to pick it up, he refuses. I tell him again he refuses. Then I say you must either pick up the handkerchief, or have a whipping. My theory is never to make a child have a whipping and pick up the handkerchief too. I say "If you do not pick it up, I must punish you." if he doesn't he gets the whipping, but I pick up the handkerchief, if he does he gets no punishment. I tell him to do a thing if he disobeys me he is punished for so doing, but not forced to obey me afterwards."

When Clara and I had been very nauty or were being very nauty, the nurse would go and call mamma and she would appear Suddenly and look at us. (she had a way of looking at us when she was displeased as if she could see right through us) till we were ready to sink through the floor from embarasment, and total absence of knowing what to say. This look was usually followed with "Clar" or "Susy what do you mean by this? do you want to come to the bath-room with me?" Then followed the climax for Clara and I both new only too well what going to the bath-room meant.

But mamma's first and foremost object was to make the child understand that he is being punnished for <u>his</u> sake, and because the mother so loves him that she cannot allow him to do wrong, also that it is as hard for her to punnish him, as for him to be punnished and even harder. Mama never allowed herself to punnish us when she was angry with us she never struck us because she was enoyed at us and felt like striking if we had been nauty and had enoyed her, so that she thought she felt or would show the least bit of temper toward us while punnishing us, she always postponed the punishment, until <u>she</u> was no more chafed by our behavior. She never humoured herself by striking or punishing us because or while she was the least bit enoyed with us.

Our very worst nautinesses were punished by being taken to the bath-room and being whipped by the paper cutter. But after the whipping was over, mamma did not allow to us leave her until we were perfectly happy, and perfectly understood why we had been whipped. I never remember having felt the least bit bitterly toward mamma for punishing me, I always felt I had deserved my punishment, and was much happier for having received it. For after mamma had punished us and shown her displeasure, she showed no signs of further displeasure, but acted as if we had not displeased her in any way.

But mamma's oppinions and ideas upon the subject of bringing up children has always been more or less of a joke in our family, perticularly since Papa's article in the Christian Union; and I am sure Clara and I have related the history of our old family paper-cutter, our punishments and privations with rather more pride and triumph, because of mamma's way of rearing us, then any other sentiment.

When the article "What ought he to have done? came out mamma read it, and was very much interested in it. And when papa heard that she had read it he went to work and secretly wrote his opinion of what the father ought to have done. He told aunt Susy Clar and I about it but mamma was not to see it or hear any thing about it till it came out. He gave it to aunt Susy to read, and after Clara and I gone up to get ready for bed he brought it up for us to read. He told what he thought the father ought to have done by telling what mamma

would have done. The article was a beautiful tribute to mamma and every word in it
true; But still in writing about mamma he
partly forgot that the article was going to be
published I think, and expressed himself
more fully than he would do the second
time he wrote it; I think the article has done
and will do a great deal of good, and I think
it would have been perfect for the family
and friends' enjoyment, but a little bit too
private to have been published as it was.
And Papa felt so too, because the very next
day or a few days after, he went down to
New York to see if he couldn't get it back
before it was published but it was too late
and he had to return without it. When the
Christian Union reached the farm and
papa's article in it, all ready and waiting to
be read to mamma papa hadn't the courage
to show it to her (for he knew she wouldn't
like it at all) atfirst, and he didn't but he
might have let it go and never let her see it,
but finally he gave his consent to her seeing
it, and told Clara and I we could take it to
her, which we did, with tardiness and we
all stood around mamma while she read it,
all wondering what she would say and
think about it.

She was too much surprised, (and pleased privately, too) to say much at first, but as we all expected publicly (or, rather when she remembered that this article was to be read by every one that took the Christian Union) she was rather shocked and a little displeased.

C. and I had great fun the night papa gave it to us to read and then hide, so mamma couldn't see it, for just as we were in the midst of reading it mamma appeared papa following anxiously and asked why we were not in bed? then a scuffle ensued for we told her it was a secret and tried to hide it; but chased us wherever we went, till she thought it was time for us to go to bed, then she surendered and left us to tuck it under Clara's matress.

A little while after the article was published letters began to come in to papa crittisizing it, there were some very pleasant ones but a few very disagreble, one of these, the very worst, mamma got hold of and read, to papa's great regret. it was full of the most disagreble things, and so very enoying to papa that he for a time felt he must do something to show the author of it his great displeasure at being so insulted. But he fi-

nally decided not to, because he felt the
man had some cause for feeling enoyed at,
for papa had spoken of him, (he was the
baby's father) rather slightingly in his
Christian Union Article

After all this, papa and mamma both
wished I think they might never hear or be
spoken to on the Subject of the Christian
Union Article, and whenever any has spoken to me and told me, "How much they
did enjoy my father's article in the Christian Union" I have almost laughed in their
faces when I remembered what a great variety of oppinions had been expressed upon
the subject of Christian Union article of
papa's.

The article was written in July or August and just the other day papa received
quite a bright letter from a gentlemen who
has read the C.U. article and give his opinion of it in these words.

It is missing. She probably put the letter between
the leaves of the Biography and it got lost out. She
threw away the hostile letters, but tried to keep the
pleasant one for her book; surely there has been no
kindlier biographer than this one. Yet to a quite creditable degree she is loyal to the responsibilities of her
position as historian, not eulogist, and honorably gives

me a quiet prod now and then. But how many, many, many she has withheld that were deserved! I could prize them; there would be no acid in her words, and it is loss to me that she did not set them all down.

I think a great deal of her work. Her canvases are on their easels, and her brush flies about in a care-free and random way, delivering a dash here, a dash there and another one yonder, and one might suppose that there would be no definite result; on the contrary I think that an intelligent reader of her little book must find that by the time he has finished it he has somehow accumulated a pretty clear and nicely shaded idea of the several members of this family—including Susy herself —and that the random dashes on the canvases have developed into portraits. I feel that my own portrait, with some of the defects fined down and others left out, is here; and I am sure that any who knows the mother will recognize her without difficulty, and will say that the lines are drawn with a just judgment and a sure hand. Little creature though she was, the penetration which was born in her finds its way to the surface more than once in these pages.

Before Susy began the Biography she let fall a remark now and then concerning my character which showed that she had it under observation. In a record which we kept of the children's sayings there is an instance of this. She was twelve years old at the time. We had established a rule that each member of the family must bring a fact to breakfast—a fact drawn from a book or from any other source: any fact would answer. Susy's first contribution was in substance as follows. Two great exiles and former opponents in war met in Ephesus—Scipio and Hannibal. Scipio asked Hannibal to name the greatest general the world had produced.

"Alexander"—and he explained why.

"And the next greatest?"

"Pyrrhus"—and he explained why.

"But where do you place yourself, then?"

"If I had conquered you I would place myself before the others."

Susy's grave comment was—

"That *attracted* me, it was just like papa—he is so frank about his books."

So frank in admiring them, she meant.

March 14th '86

Mr. Laurence Barrette and Mr. and Mrs. Hutton were here a little while ago, and we had a very interesting visit from them. Papa said Mr. Barette never had acted so well before when he had seen him, as he did the first night he was staying with us. And Mrs. _____ said she never had seen an actor on the stage, whom she more wanted to speak with.

Papa has been very much interested of late, in the "Mind Cure" theory. And in fact so have we all. A young lady in town has worked wonders, by using the "Mind Cure" upon people; she is constantly busy now curing peoples deseases in this way. And curing her own even, which to me seems the most remarkable of all.

A little while past, papa was delighted, with the knowledge of what he thought the best way of curing a cold, which was by starving it. This starving did work beautifully, and freed him from a great many severe colds. Now he says it wasn't the starving that helped his colds, but the trust in the starving, the mind cure connected with the starving.

I shouldn't wonder if we finally became firm believers in Mind Cure. The next time papa has a cold, I haven't a doubt he will send for "Miss Holden" the young lady who is doctoring in the "Mind Cure" theory, to cure him of it.

Mamma was over at Mrs. George Warners to lunch the other day, and Miss Holden was there too. Mamma asked if any thing as natural as near sightedness could be cured she said oh yes just as well as other deseases.

When mamma came home, she took me into her room, and told me that perhaps my near-sightedness could be cured by the "Mind Cure"; and that was going to have me try the treatment any way, there could be no harm in it, and there might be great good. If her plan succeeds there certainly will be a great deal in "Mind Cure" to my oppinion, for I am <u>very</u> near sighted and so is mamma, and I never expected there could be any more cure for it, than for blindness, but now I dont know but what theres a cure for <u>that</u>.

It was a disappointment; her near-sightedness remained with her always. She was born with it, no doubt; yet strangely enough she must have been four years old, and possibly five, before we knew of its existence. It is not easy to understand how that could have happened. I discovered the defect by accident. I was half-way up the hall stairs one day at home, and was leading her by the hand, when I glanced back through the open door of the dining-room and saw what I thought she would recognize as a pretty picture. It was "Stray Kit," the slender, the graceful, the sociable, the beautiful, the incomparable, the cat of cats, the tortoise-shell, curled up as round as a wheel and sound asleep on the fire-red cover of the dining table, with a brilliant stream of sunlight falling across her. I exclaimed about it, but Susy said she could see nothing there, neither cat nor table-cloth. The distance was so slight—not more than twenty feet, perhaps—that if it had been any other child I should not have credited the statement.

March 14th '86.

Clara sprained her ankle, a little while ago, by running into a tree, when coasting, and while she was unable to walk with it she played solatair with cards a great deal. While Clara was sick and papa saw her play solatair so much, he got very much interested in the game, and finally began to play it himself a little, then Jean took it up, and at last <u>mamma</u>, even played it ocasionally; Jean's and papa's love for it rappidly increased, and now Jean brings the cards every night to the table and papa and mamma help her play, and before dinner is at an end, papa has gotten a seperate pack of cards, and is playing alone, with great interest, mamma and Clara next are made subject to the contagious solatair, and there are four solatairians at the table; while you hear nothing but "Fill up the place" etc. It is dreadful! After supper Clara goes into the library, and gets a little red mahogany table, and placing it under the gas fixture seats herself and begins to play again, then papa follows with another table of the same discription, and they play solatair till bedtime.

We have just had our Prince and Pauper pictures taken, two groups and some little single ones. The groups (the Interview and Lady Jane Grey scene) were pretty good, the lady Jane Grey scene was perfect, just as pretty as it could be, the Interview was not so good; and two of the little single pictures very good indeed, but one was very bad. Yet on the whole we think they were a success.

Papa has done a great deal in his life I think, that is good, and very remarkable, but I think if he had had the advantages with which he could have developed the gifts which he has made no use of in writing his books, or in any other way for other peoples pleasure and benefit outside of his own family and intimate friends he could have done <u>more</u> than he has and a great deal more even.

He is known to the public as a humorist, but he has much more in him that is earnest than that is humorous.

He has a keen sense of the ludricous, notices funny stories and incidents knows how to tell them, to improve upon them, and does not forget them. He has been through a great many of the funny adventures related in "Tom Sayer" and in "Hucleberry Finn," <u>himself</u> and he lived among just such boys, and in just such villages all the days of his early life. "His

Prince and Pauper" is his most orriginal, and best production; it shows the most of any of his books what kind of pictures are in his mind, usually not that the pictures of England in the 16th Century and the adventures of a little prince and pauper are the <u>kind</u> of things he mainly thinks about; but that, <u>that</u> book, and those pictures represent the train of thought and imagination he would be likely to be thinking of today, tomorrow, or next day, more nearly than those given in "Tom Sawyer" or Hucleberry Finn.

Papa can make exceedingly bright jokes, and he enjoys funny things, and when he is with people he jokes and laughs a great deal, but still he is more interested in earnest books and earnest subjects to talk upon, than in humorous ones. When we are all alone at home nine times out of ten, he talks about some very earnest subject or not very often about funny things; he doesn't joke as much, tell many more funny stories than most men, when we are all alone.

He is as much a Pholosopher than as any thing I think, I think he could have done a great deal in that direction if he had studied while young, for he seems to enjoy reasoning out things, no matter what; in a great many such directions, he has greater abillity than in the gifts which have made him famous.

1st.
When we are all alone at home, nine times out of ten, he talks about some very earnest subject, (with an ocasional joke thrown in) and he a good deal more often talks upon such subjects than upon the other kind.

Thus at fourteen she had made up her mind about me, and in no timorous or uncertain terms had set down her reasons for her opinion. Fifteen years were to pass before any other critic—except Mr. Howells, I think—was to re-utter that daring opinion and print it. Right or wrong it was a brave position for that little analyser to take. She never withdrew it afterward, nor modified it. She has spoken of herself as lacking physical courage, and has evinced her admiration of Clara's; but she had moral courage, which is the rarest of human qualities, and she kept it functionable by exercising it. I think that in questions of morals and politics she was usually on my side; but when she was not she had her reasons and maintained her ground. Two years after she passed out of my life I wrote a Philosophy. Of the three persons who have seen the manuscript only one understood it, and all three condemned it. If she could have read it, she also would have condemned it, possi-

bly,—probably, in fact—but she would have understood
it. It would have had no difficulties for her on that score;
also she would have found a tireless pleasure in analys-
ing and discussing its problems.

March 21st. Sunday—Here is another of
papa's stories" told to me by Jean.

"The Generous Fender"

Once there was a night—and a pair of
tongs and a shuvel came into the library
with the other tongs and shuvels, and
pulled out the anc-anifertent fender, from
the fire-place, and began to kick it because
they didn't like it, but the fender was good;
but they went on kicking till the fender was
full of dents and spoiled. The people of the
house had gone out to a party and staid
away all night So the tongs and shuvels
kicked the poor fender till they were tired,
and then put it back in its place.

Here Jean stopped, she had forgotten
the rest of the story, and I could in no way
persuade her to go on.

March 23 '86.

The other day was my birthday, and I
had a little birthday party in the evening.

and papa acted some very funny Charades, with Mr. Gherhardt, Mr. Jesse Grant (who had come up from New York and was spending the evening with us),—and Mr. Frank Warner.—One of them was "on his knees" honys-sneeze.

There were a good many other funny ones, all, of which I dont remember.

Mr. Grant was very pleasant, and began playing the charades in the most delightful way.

Susy's spelling has defeated me this time. I cannot make out what "honys sneeze" stands for. Impromptu charades were almost a nightly pastime of ours, from the children's earliest days—they played in turn with me when they were only five or six years old. As they increased in years and practice their love for this sport almost amounted to a passion, and they acted their parts with a steadily increasing ability. At first they required much drilling; but later they were generally ready as soon as the parts were assigned, and they acted them according to their own devices. Their stage-facility and absence of constraint and self-consciousness in the "Prince and Pauper" was a result of their charading practice.

At ten and twelve Susy wrote plays, and she and Daisy Warner and Clara played them in the library or up stairs in the school-room, with only themselves and the servants for audience. They were of a tragic and tremendous sort, and were performed with great energy and earnestness. They were dramatised (freely) from English history, and in them Mary Queen of Scots and Elizabeth had few holidays. The clothes were borrowed from the mother's wardrobe and the gowns were longer than necessary, but that was not regarded as a defect. In one of these plays Jean (three years old, perhaps), was Sir Francis Bacon. She was not dressed for the part, and did not have to say anything, but sat silent and decorous at a tiny table and was kept busy signing death-warrants. It was a really important office, for few entered those plays and got out of them alive.

March 26. Mamma and Papa have been in New York for two or three days, and Miss Corey has been staying with us. They are coming home today at two o'clock.

Papa has just begun to play chess, and he is very fond of it, so he has engaged to play with Mrs. Charles Warner every morning from 10 to 12, he came down to supper/ dinner last night, full of this pleasant prospect, but evidently with something on his mind. Finally he said to Mamma in an appologetical tone, Susy Warner and I have a plan.

"Well" mamma said "What now, I wonder." Papa said that "Susy Warner" and he were going to name the chess men after some of the old bible heroes, and then play chess on Sunday.

April 18th '86.

Mamma and papa Clara and Daisy have gone to New York to see the "Mikado." The are coming home tonight at half past seven.

The other day mamma got a new rug, and she wanted to hang it up in front of the dining-room door; (aunt Clara had come two or three days before) the rug was spread out by the door, and mamma was looking at it, and comparing it with the door, to see if it was broad enough, aunt Clara seemed to think it wasn't broud enough. Mamma said "Clara I've the greatest mind to lie down and see." "Lie down and see"? "Why what do you mean Livy"? aunt Clara asked wondering. "Why I mean I've the greatest mind to lie down by the rug and see how long it is, and then get up and measure by the door." "Well aunt Clara said laughing, it seems to me that is the most orriginal way of measuring a rug, I have ever seen."

Last winter when Mr. Cable was lecturing with papa, he wrote this letter to him just before he came to visit us.

Everett House
New York Jan. 21/84

Dear Uncle,

That's one nice thing about me, I never bother any one, to offer me a good thing twice. You dont ask me to stay over Sunday, but then you dont ask me to leave Saturday night, and knowing the nobility of your nature as I do—thank you. I'll stay till Monday morning.

Your's and the dear familie's.

George W. Cable.

April 19.

Yes the Mind Cure <u>does</u> seem to be working wonderfully. papa who has been using glasses now, for more than a year, has laid them off entirely. And my nearsightedness is realy getting better. It seems marvelous! When Jean has stomack ache, Clara and I have tried to divert her, by telling her to lie on her side and try Mind Cure. The novelty of it, has made her willing to try it, and then Clara and I would exclaim about how wonderful it was it was getting better! and she would think it realy was finally, and stop crying, to our delight.

The other day mamma went into the library, and found her lying on the sofa with her back toward the door. She said "Why Jean what's the matter? dont you feel well? Jean said that she had a little stomack ache, and so thought she would lie down. Mamma said "why dont you try Mind Cure? "I am" Jean answered.

The other night papa read us a little article, which he had just written entitled "Luck," it was very good we thought.

The stories of prevailing interest, which Papa tells us is "Jim and the strainin rag" and "Whoop says I" Jim and the strainin rag is simply a discription of a little scene way out west, but he tells it in such a funny way, that it is captivating.

"Jim and the strainin Rag" "Aunt Sal!— aunt Sal! Jim's gone got the new strainin rag roun his sore schin. You Jim, take that ar strainin rag off you sore schin, an renc it out, I aller's did dispise nastiness."

"Whoop Says she."

Good morning Mrs. O'Callahan. What is it yer got in yer basket? Fish says she. They stinc says I. You lie! says she. Ter Hell says she. Whoop! says she. [and then the ingagement was on.—SLC]

Susy meant well, but in this monologue (which is from one of Charles Reid's books, I think), she has made some important omissions—among them the point of the thing. But I have suggested it in brackets. The late Mr. Bunce used to recite it in the billiard room occasionally, to relieve his feelings when the game was going against him. There was a good deal of it, and he placed the scene of it in a magistrate's court, where the speaker was explaining to the judge how a row originated and how no one was in fault but the badly battered Bridget O'Callahan, who was of a quarrelsome disposition and ever ready to take umbrage at the least little thing. Mr. Bunce threw prodigious energy and fire into the recitation, and his acting appealed to Susy's histrionic predilections. Mr. Bunce's "whoo-oop!" was the gem of the performance, and no one could do it as he did it.

"The Strainin' Rag" was a reminiscence of my boyhood-life among the slaves, and it is probable that one of its attractions for the children was, that the reciting of it was not permissible on the premises. The forbidden has always had value, for both the young and the old. Susy's way of spelling shin seems to me to lift that lowly word above the commonplace.

We all played a game of croquet yesterday evening, and aunt Clara and I beat papa and Clara, to our perfect satisfaction.

By Andrew Lang.

"Mark Twain has reached his fiftieth birthday, and has been warmly congratulated on his "Jubilee" by most of the wits of his native land. As the Ettrick Shepherd said to Wordsworth when first they met "Im'e glad you'r so young a man" so one might observe to Mark, and wish he were still younger. But his genious is still young, and perhaps never showed so well, with such strength and variety, such varacity and humor, as in his latest book "Hucleberry Finn." Persons of extreemely fine culture may have no taste for Mark, when he gets among pictures and holy places, Mark is all himself, and the Most powerful and diverting writer I think of his American cotemperaries. Here followeth, rather late, but heartily well meant, a tribute to Mark on his Jubille:

"For Mark Twain"
"To brave Mark Twain, across the sea,
The years have brought his Jubilee
     One hears it, half in pain,
That fifty years have passed and gone,
Since danced the merry star that shone
Above the babe Mark Twain."

How many, and many a weary day,
When sad enough were we, Marks way,
   (Unlike the Laureates Marks)
Has made us laugh until we cried,
And, sinking back exausted, sighed
Like Gargery Wot larks

"We turn his pages and we see
"The Missipsippi flowing free;
  We turn again and grin
  Oer all Tom Sayer did and planned
  With him of the ensanguined hand
    With Hucleberry Finn!

Spirit of Mirth, whose chime of bells,
Shakes on his cap, and sweetly smells
Across the Atlantic main,
Grant that Mark's laughter never die,
That men through many a century
May chucle oer Mark Twain!"

Susy was properly and justly proud of Andrew Lang's affectionate handshake from over the ocean, and her manuscript shows that she copied his words with grateful and pains-taking care; yet in spite of her loyal intentions she has raised his spelling to the sunny altitudes of her own, those fair heights where the free airs blow. But no harm is done; if she had asked of him the privilege she would have had it. Even to that quaint ennobling of the word chuckle, in the last line.

Mr. W. D. Howells, and his daughter Pilla have been here, to visit us, and we have enjoyed them very much. They arived Saturday at half past two and staid till Sunday night. Sunday night at supper papa and Mr. Howells began to talk about the Jews. Mr. Howells said that in "Silas Lapham" he wrote a sentence about a Jew, that was perfectly true, and he meant no harm to the Jews in saying it, it was true, and he saw no reason why it should not be recognized as fact. But after the story came out in the Century, two or three Jews wrote him, saying in a very plaintive and meek way, that they wished he wouldn't say that about them, he said that after he received these letters his consions pricked him very much for having said what he did.

At last one of these Jews wrote him asking him, to take that sentence out of the story when it came out in book form; Mr. Howells said he thought the Jews were a persecuted race, and a race already down. So he decided to take out the sentence, when the story appeared in book form.

Papa said that a Mr. Wood an equain-
tance of his, new a rich Jew who read papa's
books a great deal. One day this Jew said
that papa was the only great humorist, who
had ever written without poking some fun
against a Jew. And that as the Jews were
such a good subject for fun and funny ridicule, he had often wondered why in all his
stories, not one said or had anything in it
against the Jews. And he asked Mr. Wood,
the next time he saw papa to ask him how
this happened.

Mr. Wood soon did see papa and spoke
to him, upon this subject. Papa at first did
not know himself, why it was that he had
never spoken unkindly of the Jews in any of
his books, but after thinking awhile, he decided that, the Jews had always seemed to
him, a race much to be respected; also they
had suffered much, and had been greatly
persecuted; so to ridicul or make fun of
them, seemed to be like attacking a man
that was already down. And of course that
fact took away whatever there was funny in
the ridicule of a Jew.

He said it seemed to him, the Jews ought
to be respected very much, for two things
pertickularly, one was that they never

begged, that one never saw a Jew begging, another was that they always took care of their poor, that although one never heard of a Jewish orphans home, there must be such things, for the poor Jews seemed always well taken care of.

He said that once the ladies of a orphans home wrote him asking him if he would came to Chicago* and lecture for the benefit of the orphans. So papa went, and read for their benefit. He said that they were the most forlorn looking little wretches ever seen. He said the fact was they were starving to death. The ladies said they had done everything possible, but could not raise enough money, and they said that what they realy most needed was a bath tub. So they said that as their last resource they decided to write to him asking him to lecture for them, to see if in that way they could not raise a little money.

And they said what was most humiliating about their lack of means was that right next door, there was a Jewish orphan's home, which had everything that was needed to make it comfortable. They said

* Cleveland, not Chicago. SLC

that this home was also a work of charity,
but that they never knew, of its begging for
anything of any one outside a Jew. They
said no one (hardly) knew that it was a Jewish home, exept they who lived right next
door to it. And that very few knew there
was such a building in the city.

Stonington.
Mr. Samuel L. Clemens. May 3, 1886.
My dear Sir,
When I remember how my dear father
Dr. Todd of Pittsfield Mass. was almost
driven to dispair by the silly

Susy probably lost the rest of the letter. The rest of
her page is blank.
The following letter—evidently from Virginia—
has no date and no signature.

Soon after the war, a dear friend in Bal-
timore sent me a copy of Mark Twain's "In-
ocents Abroad" it was the first copy, that
reached the valley, possibly the first in Virginia.
All of our household read it. I lent it to
our friends, and at length nearly every body
in the village had read it.
The book was so much enjoyed by peo-

ple who were sick or sad, that it came to be considered a remedy for all cases where it could be taken, and we sent it about to people, who as the prayer book says were troubled in mind, body or estate," a discription which seemed to most Virginians in those sad and mealy days after I came to Lynchburgh the book, was sent out on its travells again, and was litterally worn out in the service. It was long past being sewed or glued, when it started on its last journey, but many of the fragments were still readable; and I tied them together again, and sent it to a nice young colored girl to read to her sick Mother to read.

I have long hoped some good Yankee, would be inspired to send me a new copy. Several of Mark Twain's books I should like much to have for my library and I think they would do a great deal of good. At one time a lady lived near me, whose daily life was so exeptionally severe and wearing, that only a woman remarkably strong in mind and body, could have stood the strain. I once lent her a copy of "Roughing it," which had been loaned to me, with permission to use it a while in my library. For a long time I could not enduce my careburdened friend to return the book, though I begged earnestly for it. She said that volume was her chief resource and comfort, when worn out with her arduous duties, and she could not do without it. A Minister to whom I chanced to repeat this remark, meaning to show the value of the book, said grimly "she had better read her bible!" I could not agree with him, as I knew my friend did not neglect her religious duties and made the bible her rule of conduct, and thought she did well to turn to Mark Twain for diversion.

May 6, '86

Papa has contrived a new way for us to remember dates. We are to bring to breakfast every morning a date, without fail, and now they are to be dates from English historie. At the farm two summers ago he drove pegs into the ground all around the place representing each king's reign following each other according. Then we used to play games running between these different pegs till finally we knew when each king or queen reighned and in refference to the kings preceeding them.

Among the principal merits of the games which we played by help of the pegs were these—that they had to be played in the open air, and that they compelled brisk exercise. The pegs were driven in the sod along the curves of the road that wound through the grounds and up the hill toward my study. They were white, and were two and a half feet high. Each peg represented an English monarch and the date of his accession. The space between pegs was measured off with a tapeline, and each foot of it covered a year of a reign. William the Conqueror stood in front of the house; 21 feet away stood the peg of William Rufus; 13 feet from that one stood the first Henry's peg; 35 feet beyond it stood Stephen's peg—and so on. One could stand near the Conqueror and have all English history skeletonized and land-marked and mile-posted under his eye. To the left, around a curve, the reigns were visible down to Runnymede; then at the beginning of a straight piece of road stood the peg of Henry III, followed by an impressive stretch of vacancy, with the peg of the first Edward at the end of it. Then the road turned to the right and came up to the end of the reign of the fifth Henry; then it turned to the left and made a long flight up the hill, and ended—without a peg—near the first corner of my study. Victoria's reign was not finished, yet; many years were to elapse before the peg of her successor would be required.

The vacancies between the pegs furnished an object-lesson; their position in the procession another. To read that James I reigned from 1603 until 1625, and William II from 1087 till 1100, and George III from 1760 till 1820 gives no definite impression of the length of the periods mentioned, but the long and short spaces between the pegs of these kings conveyed a quite definite one through the eye to the mind. The eye has a good memory. Many years have gone by, and the pegs have disappeared, but I still use them, and each in its place; and no king's name falls upon my ear without my seeing his pegs at once and noticing just how many feet of space he takes up along the road.

The other day, mamma went into the library and found papa sitting there reading a book, and roaring with laughter over it; she asked him what he was reading, he answered that he hadn't stopped to look at the title of the book." and went on reading, she glanced over his shoulder at the cover, and found it was one of his own books.

That is another of Susy's unveilings of me. Still, she did not garble history but stated a fact.

June 26, 86
We are all of us on our way to Keokuk to see Grandma Clemens, who is very feeble and wants to see us and pertickularly Jean who is her name sake. We are going by way of the lakes, as papa thought that would be the most comfortable way.

July 4. We have arived in Keokuk after a very pleasant

between these different kings till
finally we knew when each king
or queen ~~or~~ reighned & in
refference to the kings preceeding
them.—

✗

[The other. day, mamma went
into the library & found papa
sitting there reading a book,
& roaring with laughter over
it. She asked him what he was
reading. he answered that he hadn't
stopped to look at the title of the
book' & went on reading. she glanced
over his shoulder at the cover, & found
it was one of his own books.]

June 26, 86
We are all of us on our
way to Keokuk to see grandma
Clemens, who is very feeble & want
to see us & perticukularly Jean who
is her name sake. We are going

Page 130 of Susy's manuscript

y way of the lakes, as Papa
thought that would be the
most comfortable way.

July 4. We have arived in
Keokuk after a very pleasant

The last page of Susy's biography (holograph)

1

(To follow after p. 131.)

=

So ends the loving task of that innocent sweet spirit — like her own life; unfinished, broken off in the midst. Interruptions came, her days became increasingly busy with studies & work, & she never resumed the biography, though from time to time she gathered materials for it. When I look at the arrested sentence that ends the little book, it seems as if the hand that traced it cannot be far — is gone for a moment only, & will come again & finish it. But that is a dream; a creature of the heart, not the mind — a feeling, a longing, not a mental product: the same that lured Aaron Burr, old, gray, forlorn, forsaken, to the pier, day after day, week after week, there to stand in the gloom & the chill of the dawn gazing seaward through veiling mists & sleet & snow for

A page of Clemens's manuscript

PAPA

2

the ship which he knew was gone down — The ship that bore all his treasure, his daughter.

Mark Twain's final comments about Susy (holograph)

So ends the loving task of that innocent sweet spirit —like her own life, unfinished, broken off in the midst. Interruptions came, her days became increasingly busy with studies and work, and she never resumed the biography, though from time to time she gathered materials for it. When I look at the arrested sentence that ends the little book, it seems as if the hand that traced it cannot be far—is gone for a moment only, and will come again and finish it. But that is a dream; a creature of the heart, not of the mind—a feeling, a longing, not a mental product: the same that lured Aaron Burr, old, gray, forlorn, forsaken, to the pier, day after day, week after week, there to stand in the gloom and the chill of the dawn gazing seaward through veiling mists and sleet and snow for the ship which he knew was gone down— the ship that bore all his treasure, his daughter.

List of Persons

Ashcroft, Ralph W. A secretary and business manager of Clemens's late in the latter's life.

Aunt Susie. See Susan Langdon Crane.

Barrett, Lawrence (1838–1891). American actor, colleague of Edwin Booth, author of a biography of Edwin Forrest (1881).

Ben. Nickname for Clara Clemens.

Brown, Jock. Son of Dr. John Brown.

Brown, John, Dr. (1810–1882). Edinburgh physician, author of *Rab and His Friends*.

Brownell, Louise (1870–1961). A close friend of Susy Clemens from the time the two met at Bryn Mawr. For details see the Introduction.

Bunce, Edward M. A billiard-room friend of Clemens.

Burton, Richard (1861–1940). Son of Nathaniel Judson Burton, Hartford Congregational clergyman; literary editor of the Hartford *Courant;* professor of English at the University of Minnesota and later at Rollins College.

Cable, George Washington (1844–1925). American writer, author of *Old Creole Days* (1879), *The Grandissimes* (1880), *Madame Delphine* (1881), and other books. He made a lecture tour with Clemens 1884–85.

Cheneys. Frank Woodbridge Cheney and his wife, Mary Bushnell Cheney (1840–1917). She wrote a biography of her father, Rev. Dr. Horace Bushnell. Frank and his brother Knight ran the Cheney Silk Mills in Manchester, Conn.

Clemens, Clara (1874–1962). Clemens's middle daughter. She was a pianist, and until his death in 1936 the wife of Ossip Gabrilowitch, concert pianist and conductor of the Detroit Symphony Orchestra. In 1944 she married Jacques Samossoud.

Clemens, Henry (1838–1858). Clemens's younger brother, who was killed in the explosion of the Mississippi steamboat *Pennsylvania.*

Clemens, Jane Lampton (1803–1890). Clemens's mother, who was married to John Marshall Clemens (1798–1847).

Clemens, Jean (1880–1909). Clemens's youngest of three daughters. She was named Jane Lampton for her grandmother but was always called Jean.

Clemens, Langdon (1870–1872). Clemens's first child, who was born prematurely and was always frail. Clemens, with his tendency to take on guilt for the death of those close to him, blamed himself for the child's death.

Clemens, Olivia Louise Langdon (1845–1904). Clemens's wife, whom he married in February 1870.

Clemens, Orion (1825–1897). Clemens's older brother. In Clemens's opinion, a jack-of-all trades and a failure in all.

Cousin Charlie, "his agent." Possibly Charles L. Webster.

Crane, Susan Langdon (Mrs. Theodore Crane) (1836–1924). Adopted daughter of Jervis and Olivia Langdon, adopted sister of Clemens's wife. Jervis Langdon gave Quarry Farm at Elmira, New York, to the Cranes as a wedding gift.

Daisy. Margaret Warner.

Dodge, Mary Mapes. Editor of *St. Nicholas* magazine, a member of the Onteora Club, and a friend of Clemens.

Fleming, Marjorie (1803–1812). Scottish prodigy, friend of Sir Walter Scott, writer of journals and letters. Her first letter, written to her cousin Isa Keith before she was six, goes: "My dear Isa—I now sit down on my botom to answer all the kind & beloved letters which you was so so good as to write to me. This is the first time I ever wrote a letter in my life. Miss Potune, a lady of my acquaintance, praises me dreadfully. I repeated something out of Deen Swift & she said I was fit for the stage, & you may think I was primmed up with majestick Pride, but upon my word I felt myself turn a little birsay—birsay is a word which is a word that William composed which is as you may suppose a little enraged. This horid fat Simpliton says that my Aunt is beautifull which is intirely impossible for that is not her nature." Clemens wrote an essay about her, "Marjorie Fleming, the Wonder Child," which was first published in 1909.

Foote, Lilly G. (1860–1932). She became a governess in the Hartford house in 1880, when Susy Clemens was six.

George. Family butler; "that peerless black ex-slave and children's idol who came one day—a flitting stranger—to wash windows and stayed eighteen years. Until he died," Clemens wrote in *The Autobiography of Mark Twain.*

Gerhardt, Karl (1853–1940). Hartford sculptor whom the Clemenses helped to study in Paris for three years. He made busts of Clemens and Grant, as well as various statues.

Grandma Clemens. See Jane Lampton Clemens.

Grandpa Langdon. See Jervis Langdon.

Grant, Jesse. Second son of Ulysses S. Grant.

Hamersley, Miss. Possibly the daughter of William H. Hamersley (1838–1920), Hartford lawyer and judge; at one time he was a holder of stock in the Paige typesetter venture.

Harmony. Julia Harmony Cushman, wife of Rev. Joseph H. Twichell of Hartford.

Harris, Joel Chandler (1848–1908). Writer for the Atlanta *Constitution,* author of *Uncle Remus: His Songs and Sayings* (1881) and *Nights with Uncle Remus* (1883), versions of Negro folk tales.

Holmes, Oliver Wendell (1809–1894). American poet, novelist, essayist, physician, professor of anatomy at Harvard Medical School; author of *The Autocrat of the Breakfast-Table* (1858), "Old Ironsides" (1830), "The Chambered Nautilus" (1858), and other works.

Howells, Mildred H. Daughter of William Dean Howells; editor of *Life in Letters of William Dean Howells* (1928).

Howells, William Dean (1837–1920). Novelist, critic, editor of the *Atlantic,* good friend and admirer of Clemens, with whom he had a major correspondence.

Hutton, Lawrence (1843–1904). American critic, essayist, literary editor of *Harper's Magazine,* author of *Edwin Booth* (1893).

John and Ellen. Servants of the Clemenses in the Hartford house.

Lang, Andrew (1844–1912). Scottish historian, biographer, poet, folklorist, essayist, translator of Homer.

Langdon, Charles Jervis (1849–1916). Brother of Olivia Louise, Clemens's wife Livy. It was through him (Clemens and he met when they were members of the *Quaker City* Holy Land Excursion) that Clemens got to know Livy.

Langdon, Jervis (1809–1870). Clemens's father-in-law.

Langdon, Olivia Lewis (1810–1890). Clemens's mother-in-law.

Lathrop, George Parsons (1851–1898). Freelance writer, journalist, husband of Hawthorne's daughter Rose, author of *A Study of Hawthorne* (1876), and editor of Hawthorne's works in twelve volumes (1883).

Leary, Katy (1863–1941). The Clemenses' maid for many years until his death in 1910. Her memories of the Clemenses were collected and set down in *A Lifetime with Mark Twain* (1925), by Mary Lawton, a friend of Clara Clemens Gabrilowitch.

Lilly. A nickname for Elizabeth Hooker Gillette, George Warner's wife.

Livy. Clemens's wife. See Olivia Louise Langdon Clemens.

Major Pond. See James B. Pond.

Malibran, Maria Felicita (1808–1836). French-Spanish mezzo-contralto, born in Paris. She was famous for her fiery temperament as well as for the unusual range of her voice. For details see the Introduction.

McAleer, Jimmy. Son of Patrick McAleer.

McAleer, Patrick (1846–1906). The Clemenses' Irish-born coachman from 1870 until 1891, when the Hartford house was closed down. He again worked for Clemens in the summer of 1905 in Dublin, New Hampshire.

Nye, Emma. An old school friend of Livy's.

Paine, Albert Bigelow (1861–1937). Photographer, editor, biographer, close friend of Clemens from 1906 until the latter's death in 1910. Clemens's official biographer; literary editor of the Mark Twain Estate until his death.

Pilla. Mildred H. Howells.

Pond, James B. (1838–1903). Manager of Clemens's joint lecture tour with G. W. Cable in 1884–85, and of Clemens's round-the-world lecture tour in 1895–96. He had been a major in the Union cavalry in the Civil War.

Redpath, James (1833–1891). Correspondent with the Union forces in the Civil War. In 1868 he founded the Boston Lyceum Bureau, which managed lectures for Clemens and many other noted platform speakers.

Reid, Charles. A slip of the pen for Reade? Charles Reade (1814–1884) was an English playwright and novelist, author of *The Cloister and the Hearth* (1861) and other novels.

Rice, Billy. A star of the traveling minstrel show, which Clemens recalled he had first experienced probably in the early 1840s.

RoBards, John. A childhood friend of Clemens.

Robinson, Henry C. One of Clemens's billiard-room cronies.

Sage, Dean (1841–1902). A sportsman, and a New York businessman dealing in lumber.

Spaulding, Clara L. (1849–1935). A friend of Livy's, she married John B. Stanchfield, a lawyer, in 1886.

Stockton, Frank Richard (1834–1902). American author of fanciful tales; editor of *St. Nicholas* magazine. His best-known short story is "The Lady or the Tiger?" (1884).

Twichell, Joseph H. (1838–1918). Minister of the Asylum Congregational Church in Hartford 1865–1912, and a close friend and neighbor of the Clemenses, whose marriage he performed in 1870.

Uncle Charlie. See Charles J. Langdon.

Vedder, Elihu (1836–1923). American painter and illustrator.

Warner, Charles Dudley (1829–1900). Essayist, newspaper editor, novelist, good friend, and Hartford neighbor of the Clemenses, coauthor with Clemens of the latter's first novel, *The Gilded Age* (1874).

Warner, Frank. Son of George H. Warner and friend and neighbor of the Clemens girls.

Warner, George H. (1833–1919). Brother of Charles Dudley Warner and Hartford neighbor and friend of the Clemenses.

Warner, Margaret. Daisy. Daughter of George Henry and Elizabeth Warner.

Warner, Susy (Susan). Wife of Charles Dudley Warner.

Webster, Charles L. (1851–1891). He married Clemens's niece, Annie Moffett. In 1884 Clemens made him manager of his New York–based publishing firm, Charles L. Webster & Co., which published *Huckleberry Finn* and *Personal Memoirs of Ulysses S. Grant*, both in 1885.

Wheeler, Dora. American artist and the daughter of Candace Thurber Wheeler, one of the founders of the Onteora Club in the Catskills (Tannersville, New York).

Whitmore, Franklin G. (1846–1926). Clemens's business agent. He and his wife were personal friends of the Clemenses.

Wood, Mr. (Re Clemens's treatment of Jews in his writings). Possibly Charles Erskine S. Wood, adjutant at West Point.

Youth. Livy Clemens's nickname for Clemens.